# Eat & Make

sweet paul

# Eat&Make

## CHARMING RECIPES KITCHEN CRAFTS YOU WILL LOVE

## PAUL LOWE

Photographs by Alexandra Grablewski
Writing collaboration by Paul Vitale
Illustration by Susan Evenson

Houghton Mifflin Harcourt
Boston New York 2014 .

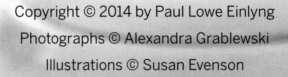

For information about permission to reproduce selections from this book, write to Permissions, Houghton Mifflin Harcourt Publishing Company, 215 Park Avenue South, New York, New York 10003.

www.hmhco.com

Library of Congress Cataloging-in-Publication Data is available.
ISBN 978-0-544-13333-4;
ISBN 978-0-544-13444-7 (ebk)

Book design by Joline Rivera and Nellie Williams

Printed in The United States of America
DOW 10 9 8 7 6 5 4 3 2 1

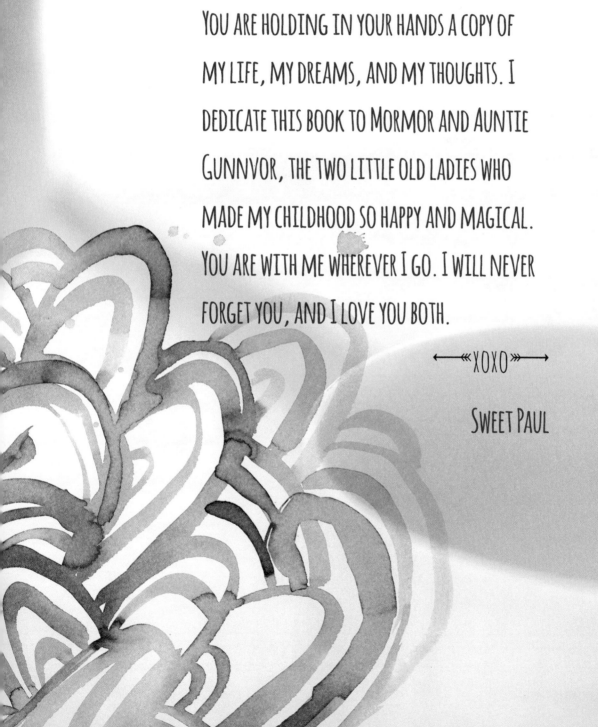

You are holding in your hands a copy of my life, my dreams, and my thoughts. I dedicate this book to Mormor and Auntie Gunnvor, the two little old ladies who made my childhood so happy and magical. You are with me wherever I go. I will never forget you, and I love you both.

←«xoxo»→

Sweet Paul

Contents

INTRODUCTION

Dear friends,

This book is about the two things in life I love the most: cooking and crafting.

I was raised in Oslo, Norway, by two little old ladies: my great-aunt Auntie Gunnvor and my grandmother Mormor. Ever since I was small, I've been obsessed with cooking, crafting, and decorating. It's in my blood. Both my grandmother and mother were excellent cooks and crafters with impeccable taste, but they were not perfectionists. Their cakes tended to be a little lopsided, and their craft projects definitely weren't up to Martha Stewart's standards. But they always had such fun!

I wasn't the typical spoiled child. I didn't whine and beg for toys and games. My tastes were a bit more sophisticated. If I wanted to go on a picnic, we went on a picnic; if I wanted to bake a chocolate cake, we baked a chocolate cake. Mormor and Auntie Gunnvor doted on me, but they also allowed me to participate in all the projects that I dreamed up. I owe them so much for inviting me into the kitchen to help and for feeding my culinary and craft inclinations at the same time that they fed my belly.

I loved helping in the kitchen. I had my own knife and cutting board, my own set of bowls, and my own space on the counter that I could reach by standing on a chair. Mormor was of the old school, and *everything* was made from scratch. Her food was rich and full of butter and cream, and we all know that tastes best. When we weren't cooking, we were always working on some creative craft project or another, finding projects in books and magazines and making our own versions at home

in the kitchen or playroom. Whether it was a recipe from a cookbook or a craft project from a kids' magazine, our creations never quite looked the same as their inspirational photos, but everything tasted wonderful and our crafts made us happy.

Now, as an adult, I've adopted my grandmother's motto, "*fullkommenhet er kjedelig,*" which means "perfection is boring," and I've incorporated it and her sheer joy of creating into everything I do. I'm quite sure that this is what allowed me to establish myself in my career as a successful food and craft stylist.

I started my blog, *Sweet Paul*, in 2008, and I would never have guessed it would grow big and turn into *Sweet Paul* magazine. I blogged about what I knew and loved: my food- and craft-styling work. Slowly but surely I started getting followers and fans from all over the world. By 2010 I had produced the first digital issue of *Sweet Paul* magazine, and because of persistent requests, we began printing the magazine and selling it across the United States, and then, in 2011, around the world. I'm living proof that magazines aren't dead.

I really don't care for visual perfection. I want the food I cook and the crafts I make to look like a real person made them. My philosophy is very simple: few ingredients, easy steps, and amazing results. With this book, you will always end up with something beautiful that will impress friends and family.

Sweet Paul

"WHY DO THEY CALL YOU SWEET PAUL?"

At least three or four times a week, I'm asked, "Why Sweet Paul?" Well, growing up in Norway I had a godmother who married an American NATO doctor in the early 1970s and moved to Texas. After only two years, she divorced him and returned to Oslo, but in that time, she had somehow managed to completely transform herself into what Mormor called a "tacky American," with big hair and tight clothes. A Peggy Bundy type—not at all like young women in Norway at the time.

Her look may have been questionable, but she was the best babysitter ever. She told me stories about living in Texas, where everything was huge. You even had to use two plates to hold a steak! I listened with big ears about rattlesnakes in the garden, huge cars, fast food, and plastic surgery. I'm sure she's responsible for my appreciation of everything American.

Somehow, over the course of her two-year stint in America, my godmother picked up an American accent that stuck with her. She would pepper conversations with American words, and I quickly became "Sweet Paul" to her. When I started my blog and had to think of a name, there was no question what it would be.

Thanks, Auntie Tove.

♥

# MORNING EAT + MAKE

When I was six years old, I woke up early one Saturday morning with an idea. I was very focused, even at an early age, and that day I knew exactly what I wanted to do.

I was going to bake cookies. By myself. I had an LP record with a cookie-baking song that I was obsessed with, a funny little ditty, "Pepperkakebakesangen"—sort of a cross between *The Cat in the Hat* and *Sesame Street*—with step-by-step instructions on how to make pepper cookies.

I tiptoed down into the kitchen with my record player. It was still dark out. I grabbed a bowl and started playing the song over and over, singing along and completing each step of the recipe. What I didn't realize was that the song was nonsense and it wasn't a real recipe at all. After an hour of work and full kilos (a kilo is 2.2 pounds!) of flour, sugar, and butter and eight eggs, I gave up. There was a giant bowl of wet cement in front of me and flour was everywhere, even on the curtains. Thank god I didn't have the wherewithal to actually turn on the oven. I'm afraid I would have set the kitchen on fire.

Worst of all, I was totally covered in a mixture of eggs, flour, and milk and I looked like I'd been battered and readied for the fryer like a big batch of fried chicken.

Suddenly I heard loud laughter from the doorway. There stood Mom, Dad, and my grandmother Mormor. They had all been awakened by the song and wondered what the heck was going on in the kitchen. I told them I was making cookies for everyone but that I had run into a few problems along the way. After a few more giggles, my mom gave me a quick rinse in the tub, while my dad cleaned the kitchen and Mormor whipped up a batch of Norwegian pancakes with blueberry jam. So much better than any old cookies!

Later that day, Mormor snuck out to the local bookstore and bought a present for me. It was my very first and my very own cookbook. It's worn and beaten, but I have it to this day.

_eat_

MORNING

Mormor's Pancakes with Homemade Blueberry Jam   16

Pumpkin Pancakes with Hot Plum Syrup   19

Baked French Toast with Strawberries & Vanilla Syrup   20

Baked Snug Eggs   25

Herb & Goat Cheese Omelet   26

Morning Biscuits with Cheddar, Dill & Pumpkin Seeds   31

Breakfast Polenta with Hazelnuts, Honey & Pears   34

Maple-Roasted Granola   37

Breakfast Churros with Cinnamon Sugar   38

4 from 1 Greek Yogurt   41

# Mormor's Pancakes with Homemade Blueberry Jam

## Serves 4 to 6

### Pancakes

- 2 cups sifted unbleached all-purpose flour (sift before measuring)
- ¼ teaspoon salt
- 3 large eggs
- 1¾ cups whole milk, plus more if needed
- 5 tablespoons butter, melted, plus more for the pan

### Jam

- 2 cups wild blueberries, fresh or frozen, (thawed, if frozen)
- ½ cup granulated sugar

Pancakes were not just a morning thing in my family, and it wasn't uncommon for us to have them for lunch or dinner. Maybe that was because Mormor's pancakes were so good. I wouldn't have minded having them for every meal in the same day! They are more like crepes than traditional American pancakes and they serve as a delicate vehicle that transports any favorite topping to your mouth.

My preferred way to eat them was with a large dollop of blueberry jam. Mormor would pick blueberries all summer and make a wonderfully simple jam that would last us throughout the year.

**1. To make the pancakes:** Place the flour, salt, eggs, milk, and butter in a food processor and process until you have a smooth batter.

**2.** Let the batter rest for 30 minutes. This will make the flour "swell" and absorb the milk so the pancakes will be easier to flip. If the batter feels too thick, add a little more milk.

**3.** Preheat the oven to 250°F.

**4.** Lightly butter a medium skillet and heat it over medium heat. Using a little less than ¼ cup batter for each pancake, pour the batter onto the skillet, swirling the pan so the batter covers the pan. Cook for 1 minute. Turn using a spatula and cook for another minute. The pancake should be light brown on each side. Keep warm on a baking sheet in the oven. Repeat with the remaining batter, adding more butter to the pan as needed.

**5. To make the jam:** In a medium bowl, stir together the blueberries and sugar. Stir until the crunchy sound of the sugar is gone, about 5 minutes.

**6.** Serve the pancakes hot, folded or rolled up around the blueberry jam.

# Pumpkin Pancakes with Hot Plum Syrup

## Serves 6 to 8

### Pancakes

2¾ cups unbleached all-purpose flour
¼ cup granulated sugar
1 tablespoon baking powder
1 teaspoon ground cinnamon
1 teaspoon ground ginger
½ teaspoon salt
1 cup canned pumpkin puree
1 large egg
2½ cups whole milk
1 teaspoon vanilla extract
Butter for the griddle

### Syrup

3 ripe plums, pitted and cut into wedges
1½ cups maple syrup

When I was a boy, I loved to watch American TV shows like *Flipper* and *The Brady Bunch*. I would marvel over the giant, fluffy towers of pancakes dripping with butter and maple syrup that appeared in practically every breakfast scene. The pancakes were so much different from the thin, delicate ones we ate in Norway. Mormor did not think they looked as delectable as I thought they did and would disapprovingly mutter, "Only in America," when she saw a stack of them.

Now that I live here, pancakes are one of my favorite dishes to make. I've not only managed to master the art of cooking a perfect stack, but of course I add my own twist. My recipe uses pumpkin puree, which gives the pancakes a deep golden color. I top them off with my plum maple syrup, an ideal marriage of tart stone fruit and dark, sweet maple, simmered until the plums are just beginning to soften. I think Mormor would approve.

**1.** Preheat the oven to 250°F.

**2. To make the pancakes:** In a large bowl, whisk together the flour, sugar, baking powder, cinnamon, ginger, and salt.

**3.** Add the pumpkin puree, egg, milk, and vanilla, whisking until combined. It is OK to have a few little lumps.

**4.** Lightly butter a large skillet and heat it over medium heat. Working in batches, use a ¼-cup dry measure to scoop out the batter onto the griddle and cook for about 2 minutes, or until you see a few little bubbles on the surface. Flip with a spatula and cook for another minute. Keep the pancakes warm on a baking sheet in the oven as you finish them. Repeat with the remaining batter, adding more butter to the pan as needed.

**5. To make the syrup:** In a small saucepan, heat the plum wedges and syrup over low heat until the plums just begin to soften, about 2 minutes; don't boil.

**6.** Serve the pancakes in stacks topped with the warm plums and syrup.

# Baked French Toast with Strawberries & Vanilla Syrup

## Serves 4

Butter for the pan
1 brioche loaf (about 1 pound)
1½ cups whole milk
4 large eggs
1 teaspoon vanilla extract
Pinch of salt
1 tablespoon granulated sugar

**Syrup**
1 vanilla bean
1 cup water
1 cup granulated sugar

Strawberries, hulled and
quartered, for serving

I had never tried French toast until my first trip to the U.S., when I visited Miami for a Norwegian magazine. After a long day on the set, the whole crew went to a diner for dinner. Everyone else ordered burgers and fries, but I spotted French toast on the breakfast menu and was intrigued. I immediately fell in love with the savory, dense egginess of the bread and the delightful and decadent sweetness of the toppings and syrup.

My version of French toast is done casserole-style. Preparing the casserole at least 1 hour in advance, or preferably the night before, gives the bread time to soak up all the goodness of the custard to ensure a dense and moist result. I top it with fresh strawberries, which pair wonderfully with my vanilla simple syrup.

**1.** Butter a 9-inch square baking dish.

**2.** Cut 6 slices of the brioche about ½ inch thick. Cut the rest into 1-inch cubes. Place the cubes in the baking dish.

**3.** Using a star-shaped cookie cutter, cut out stars (or simply use a juice glass to cut circles) from the 6 slices of bread. Place them on top of the cubes in the dish.

**4.** In a medium bowl, thoroughly mix together the milk, eggs, vanilla, and salt.

**5.** Pour the custard mixture over the brioche, pressing down gently so all the bread absorbs the liquid. Cover and refrigerate for at least 1 hour or up to overnight so the liquid is completely absorbed.

**6.** Preheat the oven to 350°F, with a rack in the middle position.

**7.** Sprinkle the top of the french toast casserole with the sugar. Bake until golden, about 35 minutes.

**8. To make the syrup:** Halve the vanilla bean lengthwise and scrape out the seeds using a small knife. Discard the pod.

**9.** In a small saucepan, bring the water, sugar, and vanilla seeds to a boil. Simmer for 5 minutes, until the sugar has dissolved and the mixture is syrupy. Cool slightly.

**10.** Serve the French toast warm, topped with the strawberries and warm vanilla syrup.

"ROAST IT, MASH IT,

BOIL IT AND LOVE IT!"

# Baked Snug Eggs

## Serves 4

- 2 medium Yukon Gold potatoes, diced
- 1 tablespoon butter, plus more for the pan
- 8 medium-thick slices good-quality smoked ham
- 2 scallions, thinly sliced
- 8 large eggs
- 4 tablespoons heavy cream
- Salt and freshly ground pepper

I'm often asked what my favorite ingredient is. I always answer the same thing: eggs! I never get tired of them; there's so much you can do with them. Runny, sunny, poached, hard-boiled, scrambled, put into omelets, on top, under, in the middle—any which way, just give me an egg, and I'm happy.

This is an awesome breakfast or brunch dish. It's so easy, fast, and tasty. The heavy cream contributes a decadent richness and the ham adds the perfect salty punch. It's also great to make for a large group, and you can even prepare everything the night before and just pop it in the oven in the morning.

**1.** Preheat the oven to 375°F, with a rack in the middle position. Butter four small gratin dishes.

**2.** Fry the potatoes in the butter in a large skillet over medium heat, stirring occasionally, until golden, 5 to 7 minutes.

**3.** Place 2 slices of ham in each dish. Divide the potatoes and scallions evenly among the dishes, then add 2 eggs and 1 tablespoon cream to each dish. Season with salt and pepper.

**4.** Bake for 15 to 18 minutes, or until the eggs are set.

**5.** Serve warm.

# Herb & Goat Cheese Omelet

## Makes 1 omelet

3 large eggs
3 tablespoons water
¼ teaspoon salt
   Pinch of freshly ground pepper
1 tablespoon butter
¼ cup crumbled fresh goat cheese
1 tablespoon chopped fresh dill
1 tablespoon chopped
   fresh chives

Once, when I was about seven years old, my parents took me to a fancy hotel in Copenhagen. It was breakfast time and I wanted a cheese omelet, since the waiter had told us that they were the specialty of the house.

I imagined a fluffy blanket of egg covered in melted cheese just like the one Mormor made for me at home. To my dismay, the omelet the waiter placed in front of me was thin and filled with goat cheese and chopped herbs. After a moment or two—or three—of hearing me complain, my mother finally got me to take a bite. To my surprise, it was a wonderfully new combination of flavors: the slight tartness of the cheese, the freshness of the herbs, and the creaminess of the eggs. From that day forward, I wanted only herbs and goat cheese in my omelets.

**1.** In a medium bowl, whisk together the eggs, water, salt, and pepper.

**2.** Melt the butter in a medium nonstick skillet over medium heat. Add the eggs and cook until they start to set, 1 to 2 minutes.

**3.** Turn off the heat. With a spatula, flip the omelet over. Sprinkle with the cheese and herbs.

**4.** Fold the omelet in half, lift it onto a plate, and serve.

CHASING THE
sweet things in life

# Morning Biscuits with Cheddar, Dill & Pumpkin Seeds

## Makes 10 biscuits

4 tablespoons (½ stick) cold butter, cut into pieces, plus more for the pan
2 cups unbleached all-purpose flour
2 teaspoons baking powder
¼ teaspoon salt
1 cup grated cheddar cheese
2 scallions, thinly sliced
1 tablespoon chopped fresh dill
1¼ cups whole milk
¼ cup raw hulled pumpkin seeds

Whenever I've got overnight guests or if I'm just treating my partner to breakfast in bed, I make these amazing biscuits. The dough is basic and yields a tender and buttery result. What really makes them sing is the sharpness of the cheddar coupled with the herbal sweetness of the fresh dill. They're topped off with the nuttiness of the raw pumpkin seeds. My favorite way to serve these is with fancy European butter like Lescure and a nice slice of cheddar or Gruyère.

**1.** Preheat the oven to 375 °F, with a rack in the middle position. Butter 10 cups of a muffin tin.

**2.** In a large bowl, mix the flour, baking powder, and salt.

**3.** Add the butter and work it into the flour mixture with your fingers; the consistency should be grainy, with some large lumps of butter and other smaller ones.

**4.** Add the cheese, scallions, dill, and milk. Mix well. The dough will be wet. Spoon it into the cups of the muffin tin. Sprinkle a few pumpkin seeds on top of each.

**5.** Bake until golden, about 30 minutes. If a toothpick inserted into the center of a biscuit comes out clean, they are done.

**6.** Cool on a wire rack before serving.

"WHENEVER I'VE GOT OVERNIGHT GUESTS OR IF I'M JUST TREATING MY PARTNER TO BREAKFAST IN BED, I MAKE THESE." — PAUL LOWE

"My philosophy is very simple: few ingredients, easy steps, and amazing results. With these recipes, you will always end up with something beautiful that will impress your friends and family." — Paul Lowe

# Breakfast Polenta with Hazelnuts, Honey & Pears

## Serves 4

3½ cups whole milk
¾ cup quick polenta
½ cup hazelnut meal (see Note)
4 tablespoons (½ stick) butter
⅓ cup honey, plus more for serving
4 ripe pears, peeled, for serving

I adore sweetened, creamy polenta for breakfast. Hazelnut meal gives this version a nice depth. The key is serving the polenta right away before it sets into a mass. I love it with nuts, honey, and pears, but you can also top it with berries, other fruit, milk, or syrup—whatever you like best. No rules here!

**1.** Bring the milk to a boil in a large saucepan.

**2.** Turn the heat down to low and slowly whisk in the polenta, stirring until smooth. Add the hazelnut meal and stir constantly until thickened, 5 to 6 minutes. Stir in the butter, then the honey.

**3.** Divide the polenta among four bowls and top each with a pear and some extra honey.

**Note:** To make hazelnut meal, toast ½ cup raw hazelnuts on a baking sheet in a 375°F oven for 10 minutes, or until they are golden brown. Rub off the skins in a clean kitchen towel. Grind the nuts in a food processor until they are finely ground.

# Maple-Roasted Granola

- 4 cups old-fashioned rolled oats
- 1 cup unsalted raw cashews
- 1 cup sliced raw almonds
- ½ cup pine nuts
- 1 cup raw hulled pumpkin seeds
- ¾ cup vegetable oil
- ½ cup maple syrup
- ½ teaspoon salt
- ½ teaspoon ground cinnamon
- ½ teaspoon ground cloves
- 1 cup dried cranberries
- 1 cup chopped dried papaya

Since I'm not a fan of anything soaked in milk, I prefer granola as a snack by itself. It's a great idea to mix a healthy snack with trashy TV—it helps balance things out. You may, of course, enjoy it with all the milk in the world and eat it while reading Proust.

No rules: Mix in whatever you like most — nuts, seeds, and dried fruits are a few of my favorites. You're looking for a nice mix of salty and sweet.

**1.** Preheat the oven to 350°F, with a rack in the middle position.

**2.** In a large bowl, mix together the oats, nuts, and pumpkin seeds.

**3.** In a small bowl, mix together the oil, maple syrup, salt, cinnamon, and cloves. Add to the oat mixture and stir well to coat.

**4.** Place on a baking sheet and bake for about 30 minutes, stirring 3 times during the cooking time, until golden.

**5.** Cool the granola completely, then mix in the cranberries and papaya.

**6.** Store in an airtight container. The granola will keep for 1 month.

# Breakfast Churros with Cinnamon Sugar

## Makes about eighteen 4-inch churros

- 1 cup water
- 2 tablespoons vegetable oil, plus more for frying
- 2½ tablespoons granulated sugar
- ½ teaspoon salt
- 1 cup unbleached all-purpose flour
- 1 large egg
- 1 cup confectioners' sugar
- 1 teaspoon ground cinnamon

The first time I tasted a churro, I was in Los Angeles with a friend and we stopped at a street cart selling Mexican food. The churros were amazing: sweet and sticky, crunchy outside and chewy inside. I had two orders and I made my friend take me to the same cart every day for the rest of my time there.

The churros are made of a basic light pastry dough, a.k.a. choux pastry. The dough is pretty hearty and sticky, yet forgiving and easy to work with. Dabbing a little bit of vegetable oil on your fingers and utensils will make handling it a breeze.

**1.** Line a baking sheet with parchment paper.

**2.** In a medium saucepan, combine the water, 2 tablespoons oil, granulated sugar, and salt. Bring to a boil and remove from the heat.

**3.** Stir in the flour rapidly, until the mixture forms a ball. Transfer to a food processor, add the egg, and process until smooth.

**4.** Put enough oil in a deep fryer or a large saucepan to reach a depth of 1 inch. Heat until a piece of the dough dropped into the oil turns golden after 30 seconds (375° to 400°F on a deep-fat thermometer).

**5.** Meanwhile, place the dough in a plastic piping bag or a ziplock bag with a corner snipped off and pipe 4-inch "sausages" of dough onto the baking sheet.

**6.** Gently transfer the dough to the oil in batches using a large spatula or slotted spoon. Fry until golden brown, about 2 minutes. Drain on paper towels and place on the baking sheet. Repeat until all the dough is used.

**7.** Mix together the powdered sugar and cinnamon in a small bowl. With a small sifter, sift the sugar mixture over the warm churros.

**8.** Serve warm.

# 4 from 1 Greek Yogurt

SERVES 1

**From 1 cup of Greek yogurt, you can make:**

**1.** 1 cup Greek yogurt + segments from 1 blood or navel orange, removed from membranes + 1 tablespoon toasted pine nuts = **Yogurt with Blood Orange and Pine Nuts**

**2.** 1 cup Greek yogurt + 1 cup fresh mixed berries + $\frac{1}{3}$ cup honey = **Yogurt with Berries and Honey**

**3.** Whir in a blender 1 cup Greek yogurt + $\frac{1}{3}$ cup pomegranate juice + $\frac{1}{2}$ ripe banana + $\frac{1}{3}$ cup blueberries = **Pomegranate Smoothie**

**4.** 1 cup Greek yogurt + $\frac{1}{3}$ cup old-fashioned rolled oats + $\frac{1}{3}$ cup raspberries = **Yogurt Parfait**

# SUNDAY MORNING

Ever since I learned to read, I have loved the morning paper. When I was a boy, I'd sit down with weak milky tea and the comic section. As an adult, I make myself a double espresso and relax in bed while reading the Sunday paper. I've been known to stay in bed the whole day reading it front to back and throwing the pages about like a blizzard of newsprint.

MORNING

*Make*

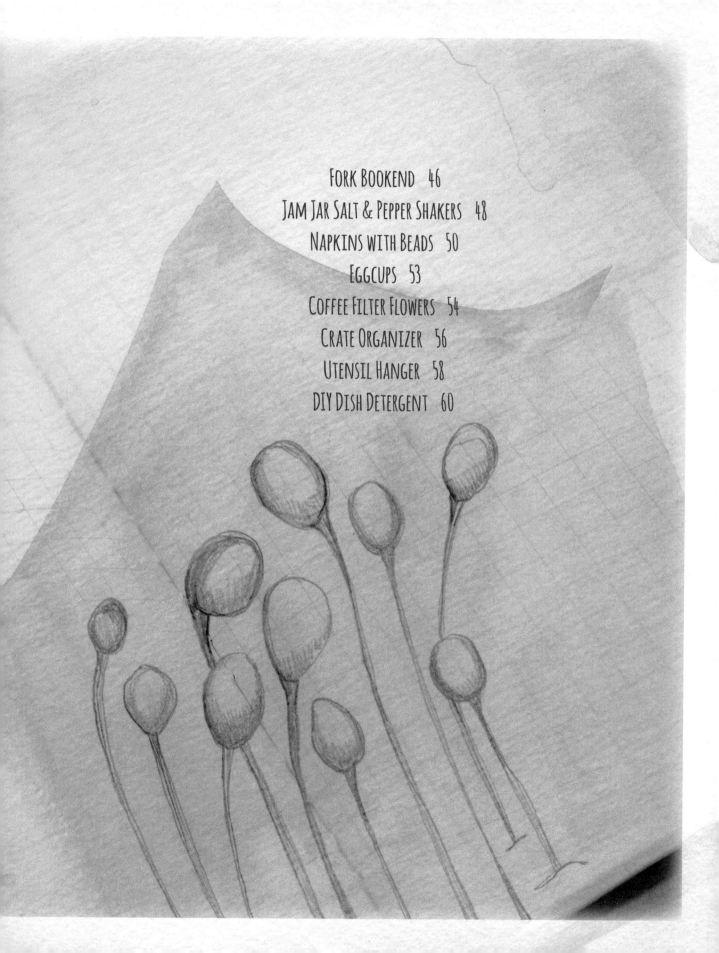

# Fork Bookend

### You will need:

Fork (I love to scour flea markets for
    old silver)
Hammer
Workbench or hammering surface—
    you can also use a vise

This simple bookend is a great way to display your favorite
cookbooks. I find it works best for a copy of *Sweet Paul Eat &
Make*, like the one you're reading right now.

**1.** Place your fork on a work surface and hammer it until it is as
flat as possible.

**2.** Bend the fork into an "L" shape. If you cannot do this by
hand, you can put the fork in a vise and use the hammer.

**3.** Grab some cookbooks and you're all set.

ENCYCLOPAEDIA
VOLUME III

# Jam Jar Salt & Pepper Shakers

## You will need:

2 small jam jars—I use
    1.5-ounce jars
Hammer
Nail
Salt and freshly ground pepper

Equally useful for the breakfast table or backyard barbecue, these salt and pepper shakers are sure to charm as well as season. If you want to take them on a picnic, simply place a piece of tape over the holes of each lid to prevent salt and pepper spills inside your picnic basket.

### Makes 1 pair of salt & pepper shakers

**1.** Remove the lids from the jars and place them on a workbench.

**2.** Using the hammer and nail, punch holes in the lids.

**3.** Fill one jar with salt and the other with pepper. Screw on the lids and go have a picnic.

# Napkins with Beads

## You will need:

About 30 small wooden beads per
napkin
Napkins—I use thin linen ones, but
you can use whatever you like
Needle and thread
Scissors

Simple wooden beads from
the craft store make these napkins
special. They add contrast and also
give the napkins a little more weight
so they stay in your lap. Note that
the embellished napkins will need to
be hand-washed after use.

**1.** Using a needle and thread, sew
the first bead onto the edge of a
napkin, looping the thread a few
times through the bead.

**2.** Sew the second bead on next to
the first.

**3.** Repeat the process until one entire
side of the napkin has a beaded fringe.
I usually just do one side, but you can
cover all four edges, if you like.

# Eggcups

Air-dry clay or polymer clay—I use
    Crayola Air-Dry Clay
Rolling pin
Cutting board
Knife
Fork

I love soft-boiled eggs, so I'm a huge advocate for the eggcup. They are disappearing from our breakfast tables, and I've vowed to reverse this process. Here's a simple project for you to make your own little pedestal for a perfect soft-boiled egg. You can also use these as napkin rings.

**1.** Roll out your clay on a cutting board to a ¼-inch thickness.

**2.** Using the knife, cut strips of clay about 1 x 4 inches. Score the strips with the fork on one side to give them an interesting texture.

**3.** Form each strip into a cylinder with a 1½-inch diameter. Pinch the ends together neatly.

**4.** Allow the clay to dry or bake it according to the package instructions.

**5.** The egg cups are ready to use.

# Coffee Filter Flowers

Bowls of water—one for each color
   you plan to use
Liquid fabric dye or food coloring—
   I always use RIT dyes
Basket-type pleated paper coffee
   filters—I usually use white, but
   you can use natural unbleached
   (not cone filters)
Scissors
Florist's wire or twist ties from
   bread bags
Display bowl

This project is a fantastic way to make a centerpiece or faux flower arrangement that you can color coordinate with any occasion or color story.

**1.** Tint the bowls of water to the desired hues with the dye or food coloring.

**2.** Separate the coffee filters into bunches and dip the edges of each bunch in a different color of dye. Set aside to dry; they dry quickly.

**3.** Cut the round, undyed bottoms off each batch of colored filters.

**4.** Cut through the remaining colored part of each filter cross-wise, so it forms a wavy accordion strip of paper.

**5.** Take a few filter strips and roll them up lengthwise into a loose tube to form the center of a flower.

**6.** Take a few filter strips of another color and continue to build the tube. You can use as many layers and colors as you'd like.

**7.** Secure the bottom of the tube with wire.

**8.** Starting with the outside of the tube, begin to spread the layers of filters and style them in the shape of a flower.

**9.** Repeat the process to make more flowers.

**10.** Style the flowers in a bowl for a bouquet.

# Crate Organizer

## You will need:

3 clementine crates
Dremel tool with a cutting
   attachment
Four 36-inch-long wooden dowels,
   $\frac{5}{16}$ inch to $\frac{1}{2}$ inch in diameter
Masking tape
Hot glue gun
Hot glue sticks

I love the graphic design of vegetable crates. Clementine crates, in particular, are bright and fun. This is a convenient organizer for tea towels and other kitchen supplies. You can also use it to hold napkins and cutlery for outside dining.

You can substitute a small saw for the Dremel tool, but the Dremel is one of the few home tool investments that I recommend. With a Dremel and a hot glue gun, you can conquer the world.

## Makes 1 organizer

**1.** Turn over the crates and inspect the bottoms. There are usually openings near the corners. If the openings are large enough to accommodate the dowels, jump to the next step. If they are too small, use the Dremel tool to enlarge the openings so they will accept the dowels.

**2.** Insert the dowels into the openings of the bottom crate. Leave about 4 inches protruding through the bottom to serve as the legs.

**3.** Using masking tape, tape the dowels in place at the top and bottom of the crate.

**4.** Using the glue gun, generously glue the dowels into each corner on the inside and allow the glue to set.

**5.** Place the middle crate about 8 inches above the bottom crate, ensure that it's level, and repeat the taping and gluing steps above.

**6.** Finish the organizer with a third crate, repeating the process used on the previous levels, and allowing the dowels to protrude about 10 inches on top.

# Utensil Hanger

## You will need:

Wire hanger
Pliers
About 14 big wooden beads
About 63 small wooden beads
Hot glue gun and hot glue sticks
    or craft glue
S-hook (available at hardware
    stores; optional)

I love to walk through the aisles of the craft store and hardware store and get inspired by the multitude of different materials. This simple project uses various-sized wooden beads and an old wire hanger that I've transformed into an object from which you can hang ladles and other kitchen tools.

## Makes 1 hanger

**1.** Untwist the wire hanger. Use the pliers to straighten out the twisty ends of the wire.

**2.** Thread the beads onto the wire, alternating size from time to time.

**3.** Once you've threaded on enough beads to get up to the neck of the hanger, bring the two ends of the hanger together and thread the remaining beads over both of the wire pieces.

**4.** Thread the beads all the way to the end and bend it into a hook shape.

**5.** Using a dab of hot glue or craft glue, seal on the last bead. Allow the glue to set, about 1 minute.

**6.** Display interesting spoons and ladles from the hanger. If you have a tool to hang that does not have a hooked end, use an S-hook to hang it.

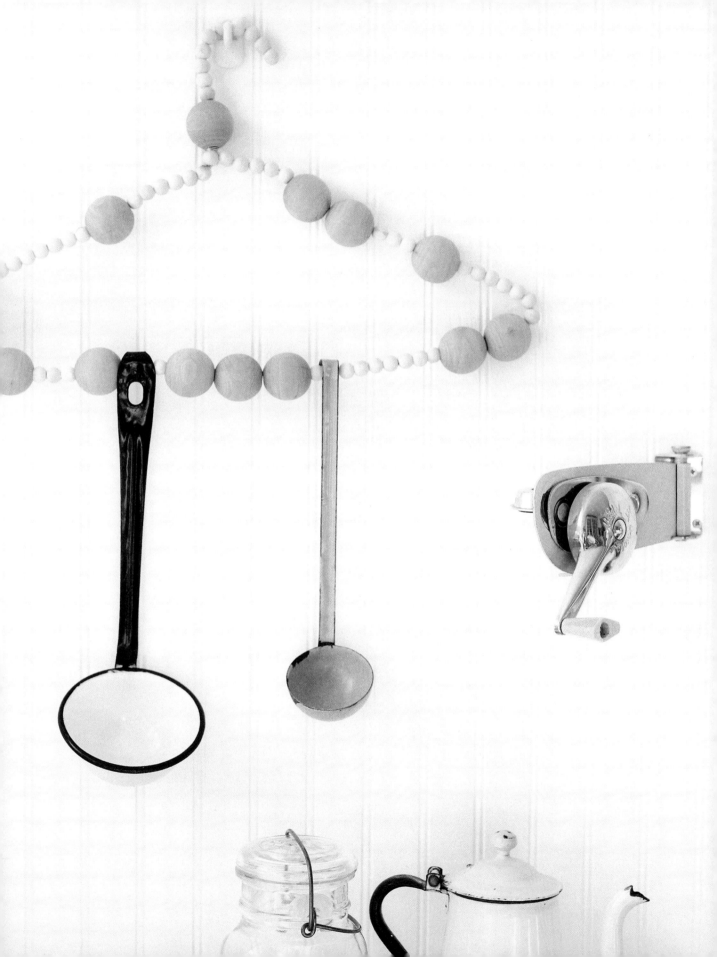

# DIY Dish Detergent

## You will need:

6 tablespoons unscented liquid
    Castile soap, such as
    Dr. Bronner's
2 teaspoons vegetable glycerin
    (available at grocery stores and
    drugstores)
5 drops essential oil—I prefer lemon
Container to hold your soap (I like to
    use an old glass jar)
2 cups water

Homemade dish soap is easy and inexpensive to make. This formula comes from my friend Sacha Dunn, the founder of the fabulous natural cleaning supply company Common Good.

Essential oils are available in health food stores, craft and candle stores, and online.

## Makes about 2 cups

**1.** Place the Castile soap, glycerin, and essential oil in your container.

**2.** Top up with the water and gently mix.

*"You go easier through life with a smile on your face."* — Paul Lowe

# BRUNCH EAT + MAKE

Ask me what my favorite meal is and I'll immediately respond, "Brunch!" I rarely eat breakfast. A double espresso with a splash of milk will usually suffice. I think it's chic and elegant to rise and have a bit of coffee and then a leisurely brunch in the late morning on the cusp of afternoon. As you can imagine, with this attitude, I was quite a handful at an early age. My parents must have been horrified when we were on holiday with friends and on being asked what I wanted for breakfast, the seven-year-old me responded, "I'm actually more of a brunch person."

When I was a boy, Mormor would try to entice me with one of her sinful breakfast creations, but I would always hold her at bay until the clock read 11:00 or 12:00. I loved this in-between time best, and I was soon able to convert her to my way of thinking. Before long she was regularly skipping breakfast and setting a brunch table in her lovely way with linen napkins and wildflower bouquets. She and I would sit and have our formal meal together. When I was an adult, she told me that I used to dab my mouth with my napkin after each bite I took. I was her Norwegian version of Little Lord Fauntleroy.

The first rule is that you can put an egg on just about anything and call it brunch. A poached egg on a kale salad? Brunch. A fried egg on a grilled ham and cheese? Brunch. Steak and scrambled eggs? Brunch. My second rule is that you can turn a dessert into a main course. Pancakes with blueberry compote? Brunch. Doughnuts in place of dinner rolls? Well, you get the idea.

When I moved to New York City, I was pleased to finally be in a city that really embraces brunch. It's available everywhere from south Brooklyn to the northern tip of the Bronx. My favorite routine is to walk to a nice brunch spot in my neighborhood with my dog, Lestat, and sit and enjoy a nice Bloody Mary, while feeding Lestat little bits from my plate. It doesn't get any better than that.

*eat*

BRUNCH

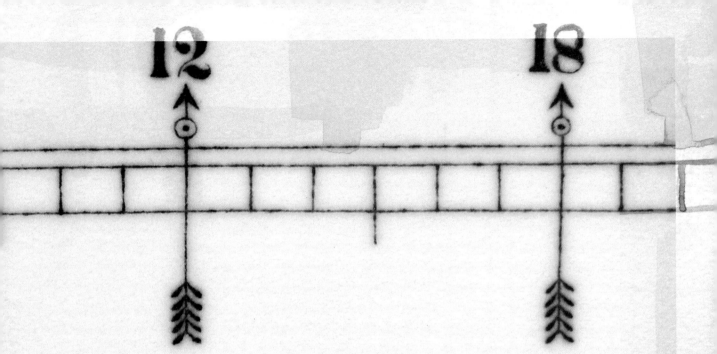

# Baked Doughnuts with Chocolate

- 8 tablespoons (1 stick) butter, melted, plus 1 tablespoon for the glaze and more for the pan
- 3½ cups cake flour
- 1 cup granulated sugar
- 1 teaspoon baking soda
- ½ teaspoon baking powder
- 1 teaspoon ground cinnamon
- 1¼ cups buttermilk, at room temperature
- 3 large eggs, at room temperature
- 1 tablespoon honey
- 6 ounces semisweet chocolate, chopped
- ½ cup unsweetened coconut, toasted (see Note)

I enjoy both cake-type and yeasted doughnuts, but when I'm making them at home, I always opt for the cake variety because they can be baked rather than fried in hot oil. High-temperature baking and a short cooking time yield light cakes with crisp golden exteriors, so these doughnuts withstand a nice dunking in milk or coffee. Using buttermilk ensures that every bite is moist, while the cinnamon and honey work together to give a warm sweetness. For an extra layer of decadence, add a quick chocolate ganache glaze and sprinkle with toasted coconut.

Doughnut pans are widely available in kitchen-supply stores. They come in two sizes, regular and mini.

**1.** Preheat the oven to 400°F, with a rack in the middle position. Grease a mini or a regular doughnut baking pan.

**2.** In a large bowl, whisk all the dry ingredients together.

**3.** In a medium bowl, mix the buttermilk, eggs, honey, and 8 tablespoons melted butter together. Add to the dry ingredients and mix until combined.

**4.** Spoon the batter into the pan, filling just a little below the rim of the molds. Do not overfill.

**5.** Bake until golden around the edges, 5 to 6 minutes for minis, 10 to 11 minutes for regular doughnuts. Cool in the pan on a wire rack for 5 minutes, then transfer the doughnuts to the rack to cool completely. Repeat until all the batter has been used, greasing the pan between batches.

**6.** Melt the chocolate and the remaining 1 tablespoon butter in the top of a double boiler or in a heatproof bowl set over a saucepan of simmering water.

**7.** Dip the doughnuts in the hot chocolate mixture, sprinkle them with the toasted coconut, and serve.

**Note: Pan-Toasting Coconut**

Heat a nonstick pan over medium heat and toast the coconut, stirring occasionally, until golden, 2 to 3 minutes. Cool.

# Auntie Gunnvor's Skillingsboller (Almond Buns)

## Makes 12 buns

### Buns
2¾ cups unbleached all-purpose flour, plus more for kneading and rolling the dough
¼ cup granulated sugar
½ teaspoon salt
1 large egg, at room temperature
1 tablespoon active dry yeast
1 cup whole milk, warmed
5 tablespoons cold butter, grated
Vegetable oil for bowl

### Filling
6 tablespoons (¾ stick) butter, softened
¼ cup granulated sugar
1 tablespoon ground cinnamon
1½ cups (10 ounces) grated marzipan
1 cup slivered almonds, toasted
1 large egg, beaten with 1 tablespoon water

My great-aunt was quite a character. She was also an amazing baker and taught me many of her baking secrets. She says these buns helped her find a husband. I'm not sure if Uncle Gunnar was drawn to Auntie because of her buns, but I know this: They sure are tasty. Her secret was adding grated marzipan. When it melts into the dough, it's just . . . well, try them yourself and see!

**1. To make the buns:** In a stand mixer fitted with a dough hook or in a large bowl with a wooden spoon, combine the flour, sugar, salt, egg, yeast, and milk and mix well until the dough comes together.

**2.** Knead the dough for about 10 minutes in the mixer or turn it out onto a lightly floured work surface and knead for 15 minutes by hand. If it feels too sticky, add more flour, 1 tablespoon at a time.

**3.** If necessary, turn the dough out onto a lightly floured surface. Add the grated butter, little by little, kneading it into the dough until it is all incorporated and the dough is smooth and elastic.

**4.** Place the dough in a large oiled bowl, cover with a towel, and place in a warm spot. Let rise until doubled, about 1 hour.

**5.** On a lightly floured surface, roll the dough out with a rolling pin into a 12-x-16-inch rectangle.

**6. To make the filling:** Spread the dough with the butter. Sprinkle the sugar, cinnamon, marzipan, and almonds evenly over the butter.

**7.** Roll the dough up along the long side into a log and cut it into 12 equal pieces.

**8.** Place the pieces on a baking sheet about ½ inch apart, cover with parchment paper, and let rise in a warm spot for 1 hour, or until doubled in size.

**9.** About 20 minutes before you plan to bake, preheat the oven to 350°F, with a rack in the middle position.

**10.** Brush the rolls with the egg wash and bake for 20 minutes, or until golden brown.

**11.** Cool on a wire rack and serve.

# Breakfast Pizza with Pancetta, Eggs & Potatoes

## Makes 4 individual 6-inch pizzas

1 cup warm water (110°F)
1 tablespoon honey
1 teaspoon active dry yeast
2¾ cups unbleached all-purpose flour, plus more for kneading and rolling the dough
2 tablespoons olive oil, plus more for the bowl
Salt
2 large potatoes, diced
8 ounces pancetta, diced (2 cups)
4 large eggs
Freshly ground pepper
4 scallions, thinly sliced

Yes, you can have pizza for breakfast! Kids of all ages love this idea.

This is my go-to pizza dough recipe, versatile and easy to learn by heart. I usually make personal pizzas so that everyone can top them the way that they want, and I always encourage everyone to leave some room in the middle for an egg. If you feel extra adventurous, try the pizza with duck eggs: It's amazing.

**1.** Preheat the oven to 400°F, with racks in the lower and upper thirds. Line two baking sheets with parchment paper.

**2.** In the bowl of a stand mixer fitted with a dough hook or in a large bowl with a wooden spoon, mix the warm water and honey. Add the yeast and let stand for 5 minutes, or until bubbly. (If it does not form bubbles, start over with new yeast.)

**3.** Add the flour, oil, and ½ teaspoon salt and mix to combine. Knead the dough for 5 minutes in the mixer or turn it out onto a lightly floured surface and knead for 10 minutes by hand.

**4.** Place the dough in an oiled large bowl, cover, and let rise in a warm spot until doubled in size, about 45 minutes.

**5.** Divide the dough into 4 parts. Dust the workspace with a little flour and roll out each piece into a free-form 6-inch circle. Place on the baking sheets.

**6.** Place the potatoes in a large saucepan of salted water and bring to a boil. Cook until soft, 18 to 20 minutes. Drain completely and scatter the potatoes on the pizzas.

**7.** Meanwhile, cook the pancetta in a large skillet over medium heat until golden, 5 to 7 minutes. Top the pizzas with the pancetta and drizzle each pizza with some of the fat from the pan.

**8.** Bake the pizzas for 5 minutes. Remove from the oven and crack an egg on top of each pizza. Sprinkle with salt and pepper.

**9.** Return the pizzas to the oven and bake, rotating the pans once during baking, until golden and the eggs are set, 10 to 12 minutes more.

**10.** Sprinkle with the scallions and serve.

SWEET AS A CARROT

# Croque Madame

## SERVES 4

2 tablespoons butter

1½ tablespoons unbleached all-purpose flour

1½ cups whole milk, warmed, plus more if needed
Salt and freshly ground pepper

8 slices brioche bread, sliced ½ inch thick (you can substitute challah or a good Pullman loaf)

8 slices ham (about ½ pound)

8 ounces grated Gruyère cheese (2 cups)

4 large eggs, fried sunny-side up

One summer, when I was young, we rented a house on the small island of Île de Ré, off the west coast of France. Along the way, a three-day drive from Oslo, through Denmark and Germany, we stopped at every flea market we could find to feed my parents' treasure-hunting addiction. (To this day, I can't pass up a flea market no matter how hard I try.)

One afternoon, we stopped at a roadside café. I didn't understand a word of French, but I pretended to read the menu in a worldly manner. I zeroed in on a sandwich that I guessed was ham and cheese. What emerged from the kitchen was made with thick pieces of bread, covered with ham and melted cheese, and topped with a sunny-side-up egg. Heaven. Since that day, Croque Madame has been my favorite lunch.

**1.** Preheat the oven to 400°F, with a rack in the middle. Cover a baking sheet with parchment paper.

**2.** Melt the butter in a small saucepan and add the flour. Stir constantly for about a minute; do not let the mixture get dark.

**3.** Add the milk, a little at a time, stirring with a whisk until you have a smooth sauce. If it's too thick, just add some more milk. Season with salt and pepper to taste and scrape the sauce into a shallow bowl.

**4.** Dip each of 4 pieces of bread into the sauce, then place the bread on the baking sheet.

**5.** Top each slice of bread with 2 slices of the ham and some of the cheese.

**6.** Dip the remaining 4 slices of bread and place one on top of each of the sandwich bottoms.

**7.** Top with the remaining cheese.

**8.** Bake until golden, about 15 minutes.

**9.** Serve hot, with a fried egg on top of each.

# Morning Tart with Broccoli, Goat Cheese & Smoked Salmon

Serves 4

Butter for the pan
Salt
1 broccoli crown, cut into small florets (about 2 cups)
1 sheet puff pastry, thawed
1 small red onion, cut into thin slices
½ cup crumbled fresh goat cheese
4 large slices smoked salmon, cut into pieces
1 tablespoon chopped fresh dill

Puff pastry is my secret weapon: I always make sure I have a package of Dufour puff pastry in the freezer. It's easy to work with and you can make so many cool things with it. The flaky layers look beautiful even if you're not a master pastry chef—and I'm not. It's especially great for tarts: You just roll it out and top it with whatever you want.

This morning tart is one of my preferred ways to use puff pastry. You can make it as one big tart on a baking tray or as a smaller tart (as I do here) or even as individual portions. These toppings are suggestions. You can use whatever you love the most or have on hand.

**1.** Preheat the oven to 400°F, with a rack in the middle position. Butter a 9-inch round baking dish or ovenproof skillet.

**2.** Bring salted water to a boil in a medium saucepan, add the broccoli, and cook for 1 minute. Drain and immediately place the broccoli in a bowl of cold water. Drain again.

**3.** Place the puff pastry in the baking dish; it's fine if some hangs over the edges. If it's too big, trim the sides with a sharp knife.

**4.** Top with the blanched broccoli, onion, and goat cheese.

**5.** Bake until golden and puffed, 18 to 20 minutes.

**6.** Remove from the oven and top with the salmon and dill. Serve warm.

# Benedict Goes to Norway

Serves 4

1 tablespoon butter
5 ounces baby spinach
Salt and freshly ground pepper
4 slices white bread, toasted
8 large slices smoked salmon
2 tablespoons white vinegar
4 large eggs

Nearly every meal—and certainly every party or gathering—in Norway includes at least one smoked salmon dish. In fact, when I was growing up, it seemed as though we ate salmon morning, noon, and night. In my travels throughout the United States, I've found great smoked salmon everywhere, and I still eat it all the time.

This is my take on classic eggs Benedict. It's so much tastier made with smoked fish than Canadian bacon. Search out wild smoked salmon, since it's much leaner than farm-raised and has much better flavor.

**1.** Bring a large pot of water to a simmer.

**2.** Melt the butter in a medium saucepan over medium-high heat. Add the spinach and stir until it's wilted, 1 to 2 minutes. Season with salt and pepper.

**3.** Divide the spinach among the toasts and top each with 2 slices of the salmon.

**4.** Add the vinegar to the simmering water.

**5.** Crack an egg into a cup and gently slide it into the water. Repeat with another egg. Simmer until the whites are set, 2 to 3 minutes. Remove the poached eggs with a slotted spoon and place on paper towels. Trim away the ragged white pieces and discard. Poach the remaining 2 eggs.

**6.** Place a poached egg on top of each salmon toast, sprinkle with pepper, and serve right away.

along the way we stopped at every flea market we could find.

# Smoked Salmon Hash with Scallions, Dill & Eggs

## Serves 4

- 2 medium Yukon Gold potatoes, cut into ¾-inch cubes
- Salt
- 2 tablespoons butter
- 1 small red onion, finely chopped
- 3 scallions, thinly sliced
- Freshly ground pepper
- Pinch of red pepper flakes (optional)
- 2 tablespoons white vinegar
- 4 large eggs
- 6 slices smoked salmon, cut into pieces
- 1 tablespoon chopped fresh dill

Hash is a versatile recipe that's great to have under your belt. You can make a hash out of just about any meat or fish, and it's a great way to deal with leftovers. This recipe combines traditional Scandinavian flavors of dill, salmon, and potatoes in a nontraditional hash. When you top the hash with a poached egg, the rich yolk serves as a sauce. You'll want to make this again and again.

**1.** Place the potatoes in a medium saucepan of salted water and bring to a boil. Cook until almost done, 8 to 10 minutes. Drain.

**2.** Melt the butter in a medium skillet and add the onion and scallions. Cook, stirring, until the onion softens, 3 to 4 minutes.

**3.** Add the parcooked potatoes to the skillet and cook until golden, about 4 minutes. Season the hash with salt, pepper, and, if you like, some red pepper flakes.

**4.** Meanwhile, bring a large pot of water to a simmer.

**5.** Add the vinegar to the simmering water.

**6.** Crack an egg into a cup and gently slide it into the water. Repeat with another egg. Simmer until the whites are set, 2 to 3 minutes. Remove the poached eggs with a slotted spoon and place on paper towels. Trim away the ragged white pieces and discard. Poach the remaining 2 eggs.

**7.** Add the salmon and dill to the hash and serve with the poached eggs on top.

*"Give me some eggs and I'm a happy camper." — Paul Lowe*

# Smoked Trout Salad with Hard-Cooked Eggs

### Serves 4

- 1 whole smoked trout or mackerel, bones and skin removed, or 8 ounces canned
- 3 tablespoons mayonnaise, plus more if needed
- 1 tablespoon chopped fresh dill
- 1 tablespoon finely chopped celery
- 1 tablespoon finely chopped red onion
- 1 scallion, thinly sliced
- 1 tablespoon fresh lemon juice
  Salt and freshly ground pepper
- 1 hard-boiled egg, cut into quarters, for serving
- 4 slices Finnish Rye Bread (page 87) or other dark rye bread, for serving

Ever since I was a kid, I've loved salted and smoked fish, especially mackerel. I grew up with this dish as a breakfast treat, and I often make it with smoked trout, since it's readily available. When you combine smoked fish with onion and celery and an egg, the result is a dish that's fresh, healthy, and delicious.

**1.** Place the trout or mackerel in a bowl and use a fork to flake the flesh.

**2.** Add the remaining ingredients except the salt and pepper and mix well. If the salad seems too dry, add some more mayonnaise. Season with salt and pepper.

**3.** Serve on rye bread, with a wedge of hard-boiled egg on top of each serving.

# Finnish Rye Bread

## Makes 1 loaf

- 1 package active dry yeast
- 1¼ cups warm water (110°F)
- 1 tablespoon dark brown sugar
- 1 tablespoon vegetable oil, plus more for the bowl
- 2 teaspoons salt
- 1¼ cups rye flour
- 1½ cups unbleached all-purpose flour
- Butter, softened, for the pan and the loaf

For me, rye bread needs to be chewy, but not too dense, and it should be moist. This recipe, which took me years to perfect, delivers on both every time. Brushing the loaf with butter gives the crust that extraspecial taste and texture I want. I love slices of this bread with good butter and Jarlsberg.

**1.** Dissolve the yeast in the water in the bowl of a stand mixer or in a large bowl. Let stand for 5 minutes, or until bubbly. (If it does not form bubbles, start over with new yeast.)

**2.** Add the brown sugar, oil, salt, and rye flour and mix or stir with a wooden spoon until smooth.

**3.** Stir in 1 cup of the all-purpose flour and mix well; the dough will still be a bit wet.

**4.** Pour the remaining ½ cup all-purpose flour out on a work surface and knead the dough until it is very smooth, about 5 minutes.

**5.** Place the dough in a well-oiled bowl, cover, and let rise in a warm spot for 1 hour, or until doubled. Butter a 9-x-4-inch loaf pan.

**6.** Knead again for a minute. Place the dough in the loaf pan, cover, and let rise for another hour.

**7.** About 20 minutes before you plan to bake, preheat the oven to 375°F, with a rack in the middle position.

**8.** Bake until golden, about 35 minutes. The bread is done when it makes a hollow sound when you knock on it.

**9.** Brush the top of the loaf with softened butter. Invert the pan and turn out the loaf, then turn the loaf right side up and cool on a wire rack.

PAINT

not ...
on to Auntie ...
..., but I knew tha... ...
tasty. Her secret was adding
grated marzipan. When it melts
into the dough, it's just... well,
...m them yourself and see.

# Herring & Beet Salad

2 medium Yukon Gold potatoes,
  peeled and cubed
  Salt
1½ cups cubed pickled beets,
  drained
1 cup cubed plain pickled herring,
  (one 8.8-ounce jar) drained
½ apple, cubed
½ small red onion, finely chopped
2 hard-boiled eggs, cubed
¼ cup white vinegar
2 tablespoons water
2 tablespoons sugar
  Rye bread, preferably Finnish
  Rye Bread (page 83), for
  serving

My father was famous for this salad, and justly so. He would make big batches every week, but somehow it would never be enough. The combination of salty herring and sweet apple and earthy beets creates an amazing harmony of flavors. It's the salad I make whenever I'm homesick.

**1.** Place the potatoes in a medium saucepan of salted water and bring to a boil. Cook the potatoes until soft, 5 to 6 minutes. Drain.

**2.** In a large bowl, mix the potatoes, beets, herring, apple, onion, and eggs.

**3.** In a small saucepan, bring the vinegar, water, and sugar to a boil. Boil for 1 minute, stirring, then cool.

**4.** Stir the cooled vinegar mixture into the salad.

**5.** Let the salad stand for a few hours in the fridge so the flavors mellow before serving it on rye.

# The Merry Mary

**MAKES ONE 10-OUNCE COCKTAIL**

3   large very ripe heirloom
     tomatoes, sliced in half (about
     3 pounds)
1   ounce fresh lime juice
1   teaspoon freshly grated or
     bottled horseradish
     Tabasco
     Generous pinch each of salt and
      freshly ground pepper
2   ounces vodka
     Slice of cucumber, for garnish
     Slice of lime, for garnish

Crush ripe summer tomatoes, then strain them, and you're left with the intense essence of tomato. It's the key to my light and refreshing take on a Bloody Mary—the Merry Mary. This mixed drink is a perfect segue from your brunch to afternoon cocktails.

**1.** Use your hands to crush the tomatoes into a bowl. Discard the solids and strain out the seeds. You should have about 1 cup juice.

**2.** Pour the tomato juice into a tall glass. Stir in the lime juice, horseradish, Tabasco to taste, and salt and pepper. Chill for 1 hour.

**3.** Add ice and stir in the vodka. Garnish with the cucumber and lime slices and serve.

was an amazing baker and taught
many of her baking secrets. She sa
these buns helped her find a husb...
I'm not sure if Uncle Gunnar was d...
...Auntie because of her buns, but t...

Some years ago, on a trip to San Francisco, I passed a secondhand clothing store and there, in the window, was an old Louis Vuitton train case. I went inside and inquired about it. According to the shopkeeper, it had belonged to a rich old lady who went on cruises all the time. The rumor was that she didn't keep an apartment anymore—she just hopped from ship to ship all year long.

The case is now my food-styling kit. It's full of knives, tongs, sprays, tweezers, and all the secret tools and ingredients of a food stylist. I've even heard that the case has gotten me jobs. If someone can't remember my name, he or she will say, "The guy with the Louis Vuitton case."

# make

# Felted Vase

## You will need:

Felting wool (available at yarn and
    craft stores)
A glass vase or jar
Dishwashing liquid

I have so much fun with felting projects, and once you know the process, you'll want to cover everything with felt. The result always looks beautifully organic. In this project, I transform ordinary, inexpensive vases into something special. Make these in a rainbow of colors so you can match them to different settings and fill them with different flowers.

**1.** Pull a piece of wool from the skein.

**2.** Begin to wrap the vase with lengths of the fibers, small handfuls at a time, ensuring that the lengths wrap completely around the vase.

**3.** Tightly add more layers, bit by bit, alternating the direction of the layers so the fibers crisscross one another. The layers will grab one another like Velcro.

**4.** Repeat this process until you have about ¼-inch thickness of wool around the vase. Make sure you cover the bottom as well using the same technique. The felt fibers will look like a coating of cotton candy.

**5.** Over the sink, drizzle about a teaspoon of dish washing liquid all over the wool on the vase.

**6.** Turn on the hot water and slowly drip it over the soapy wool, gently patting and massaging the felt until the whole piece is sudsy and the fibers mat together. This may take up to 15 minutes.

**7.** Turn the water to hot and slowly rinse the suds away. The wool fibers will shrink and tighten on the vase. (If the fibers do not shrink, use boiling water—carefully!—from a teakettle.)

**8.** Repeat the last step with cold water.

**9.** Repeat the sudsing and rinsing 2 or 3 more times with hot and cold water.

**10.** Squeeze out as much of the water as you can from the felt and set the vase aside to dry completely, usually about 3 hours.

# Hanging Colander Basket

## YOU WILL NEED:

5 S-hooks (I use 1.75-inch hooks)
Colander with two handles (mine
    is vintage, but you can use a
    vintage-style or new one)
Four 2-foot lengths of chain
1 ceiling hook

Hanging baskets are useful for storing onions, potatoes, or other produce. I made mine in minutes from a colander I found at a flea market. Chains are available at hardware stores.

**1.** Place an S-hook on one end of each length of chain.

**2.** Using the S-hook, hook a chain to one side of each of the colander's handles.

**3.** Join all four lengths of chain at the top with the remaining S-hook.

**4.** Hang the basket from a hook.

# Pie Tin Tiered Cookie Stand

## You will need:

3 vintage pie tins in three different
    sizes (I use 9-inch, 5-inch, and
    3-inch)
Glue for bonding wood to metal
    (I use Gorilla Glue)
2 wooden spools, one taller than the
    other (I use 5-inch and 4-inch)

The patina on this three-tiered dessert server gives it a vintage feel. Use it to display homemade cookies at the next potluck and you'll be the talk of the party. The pie tins are easy to find at any flea market.

**1.** Begin by placing the largest pie tin on a work surface. Use glue to attach one end of the taller wooden spool to its center.

**2.** Let the glue set for 5 minutes. Apply more glue to the top of the spool and stick the medium pie tin on top. Let the glue set. Repeat with the shorter spool and smallest tin.

**3.** Allow the glue to set according to the package instructions. Fill with cookies.

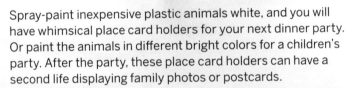

# Animal Place Card Holders

## You will need:

Dremel tool with a cutting disk
Cute plastic animals
White spray paint
Place cards

Spray-paint inexpensive plastic animals white, and you will have whimsical place card holders for your next dinner party. Or paint the animals in different bright colors for a children's party. After the party, these place card holders can have a second life displaying family photos or postcards.

**1.** Using the Dremel tool, carefully cut a narrow slot in the back of each animal, making sure the slots are deep enough to hold the cards upright.

**2.** Spray-paint the animals. I use at least two coats to ensure the plastic is completely covered.

**3.** Allow the animals to dry, insert the place cards, and enjoy your party.

# No-Sew Apron

### You will need:

Hammer
2-inch grommets
Kitchen towel
Thin cotton rope
Scissors
2 lobster clasps or carabiners

The hardware and rope make this apron suitable for both men and women. They're great to have around when someone offers to help with the dishes, and they make wonderful housewarming gifts. There's a vast variety of tea towels to choose from. You can find the lobster clasps or carabiners in hardware stores.

**1.** Using a hammer, put the grommets into the two corners of a long side of the kitchen towel, according to the manufacturer's instructions.

**2.** Cut 2 lengths of cotton rope. I keep them long so I can wrap them around my waist at least once before tying.

**3.** Tie the cords to the clasps and fasten the clasps through the grommets. Ready to wear!

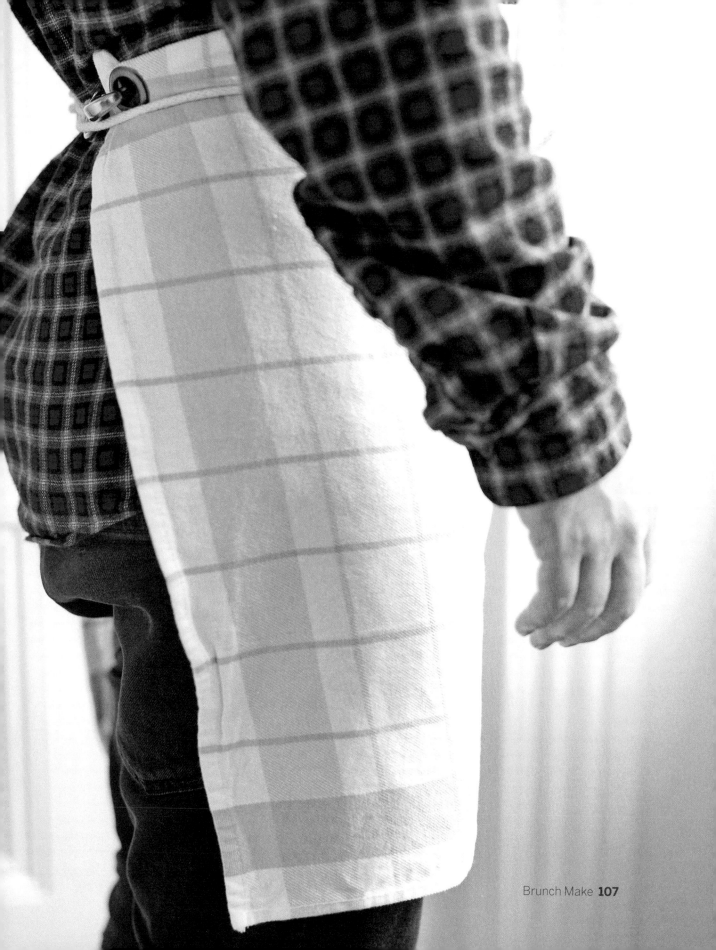

# Market Bag

### You will need:

Textile paint pen (I prefer to use
    Hermès orange, but you can use
    whatever color you want)
Plain canvas market tote

In Norway, people rarely use plastic bags for groceries: They use canvas or mesh bags. I put my own spin on my totes to make them stand out.

Canvas totes are widely available in craft stores. If you don't have a paint pen, you can use regular fabric paint and a pencil eraser. (Dip the eraser in the paint and stamp out the dots.)

**1.** Use the paint pen to stamp out a design onto your bag. I like polka dots, which are easy.

**2.** Let the paint dry and you are ready to shop.

# Natural Dip-Dyed Tablecloth

## You will need:

White or light-colored tablecloth
    made of cotton or linen
1 gallon pure black currant juice
¼ cup white vinegar
Large pot

You don't need to purchase chemical dyes when there are so many natural opportunities within the aisles of the supermarket. Dipping fabrics in coffee will dye them light brown; tea makes linens looked aged; turmeric lends a bright orange hue; a pot of boiling red cabbage creates a pretty bluish red. In this project, black currant juice turns the tablecloth a luxurious dark pink.

**1.** Prewash the tablecloth and leave it wet.

**2.** Heat the black currant juice and vinegar in the large pot to a near boil.

**3.** Dip one or more of the sides of the wet tablecloth into the dye. If it doesn't look dark enough, dip it again. Remember that it will look lighter when it dries. Rinse in warm water.

**4.** Hang to dry and it's ready to use. Hand wash in cold water.

# NOON EAT + MAKE

When I was a boy, I had one wish, and that was to grow up to become a flight attendant. This was in the 1970s, when people still dressed up for airline travel and flying was still chic. My room was filled with posters of airliners. Not just any airliners: They were all Air France. My family and I had once flown first class on an Air France 747 from Paris to Spain.

All the stewardesses had bob haircuts and were beautifully dressed. My mom told me that their clothes were designed by Balenciaga. I was in love with them. From that day on, I wanted to work for Air France, in first class, with a Balenciaga uniform. I was so obsessed with the idea that I built an airline cabin in the basement. I made the seats from our old dining room chairs, equipping them with seat belts fashioned from my dad's old belts. I built the galley kitchen out of cardboard boxes.

I would play down there for hours, filling the seats with my teddy bears and dolls. Mormor did the luncheon catering, and not just tea and biscuits, either. I requested trays of canapés and tea cakes, and fizzy soda, which I served as Champagne. She would put the food on our finest silver trays—this was first class, after all. When all my toys were seated and securely fastened in, I closed the door to the basement like an airplane door and recited my welcome announcement:

"*Bonjour, mesdames et messieurs*, I'm Paul, your head steward. Welcome to this Air France Boeing 747 bound for Tokyo, Japan. Flight time is seventeen hours. Fasten your seat belts and enjoy your flight. *Bienvenue!*"

As I grew older, my family and friends indulged my obsession by bringing me gifts from their flights. I had china, glasses, flatware, safety cards, playing cards, cutlery, and in-flight magazines galore. I almost fainted when a friend of my parents gave me a plate from the Concorde! To this day, I think back to the delicious food Mormor made for my basement airplane. And you better believe that I treat myself to flying first class every chance I get!

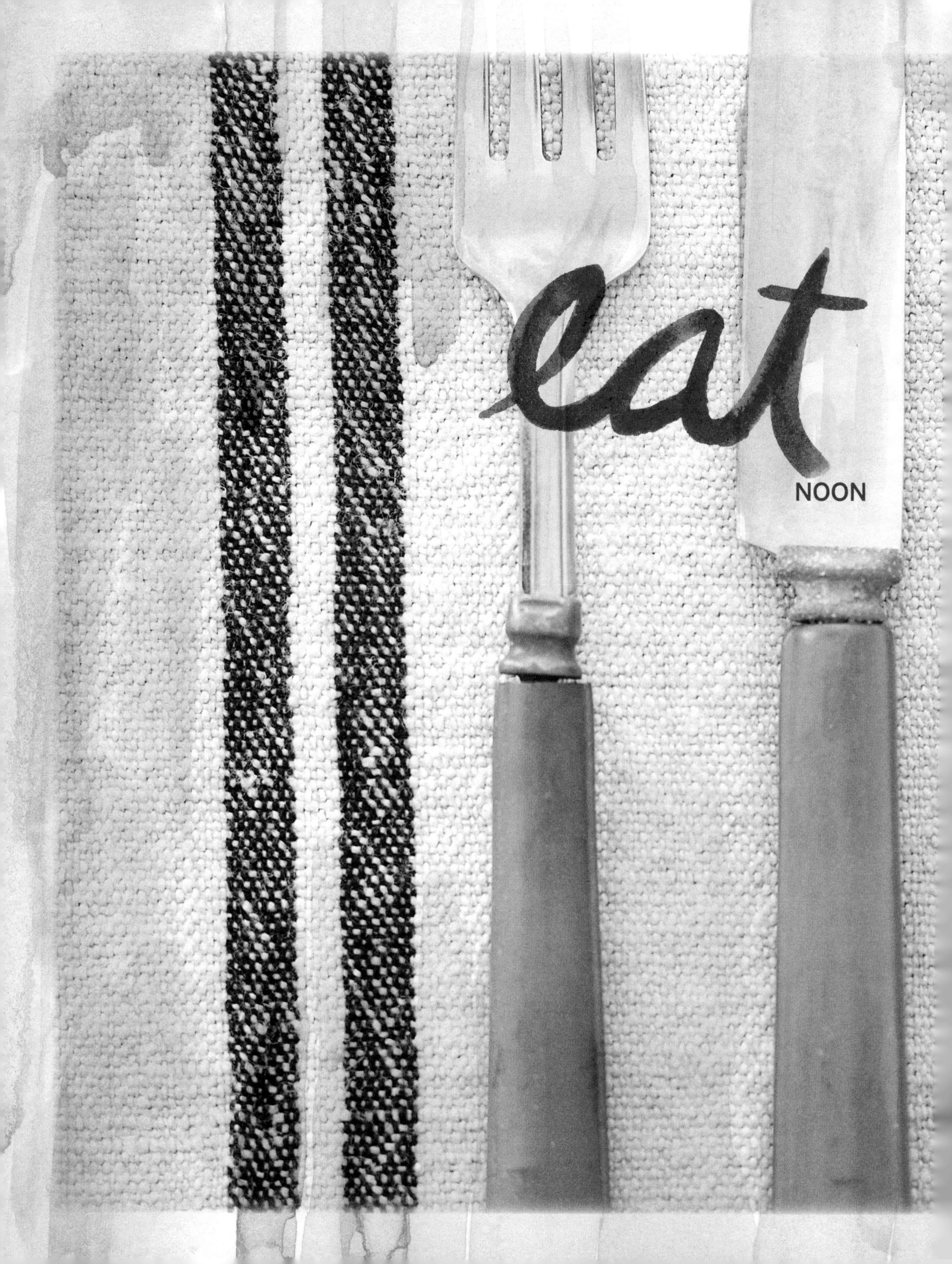
eat
NOON

# Feta & Lemon Dip

Serves 4

7   ounces feta cheese (about 1 cup
    crumbled)
1   tablespoon grated lemon zest,
    plus more for garnish
1–2 tablespoons fresh lemon juice
1   garlic clove, minced
6   tablespoons extra-virgin olive
    oil, plus more for serving
    Pinch of red pepper flakes
    Crudités, chips, toasts, or pita
    crisps, for serving

This is the most blogged, tweeted, and pinned recipe I have ever created. I came up with it years ago and then forgot all about it until I was looking through an old cooking notebook of mine. It's a surefire crowd-pleaser.

It's also one of the simplest recipes ever. Just a few ingredients, 2 minutes in the food processor, and *voilà*, you have the most amazing dip. I've even used it as a topping for baked chicken or white fish.

**1.** Place the feta, lemon zest, 1 tablespoon lemon juice, garlic, and olive oil in a blender and whir until combined but still slightly chunky. It's dense, so you may need to stir it with a fork once or twice. Taste, and if it's too salty, add more lemon juice.

**2.** Spoon into a serving bowl, drizzle with a little oil, and sprinkle with a pinch of red pepper flakes and some lemon zest.

**3.** Serve with crudités, chips, toasts, or pita crisps.

# Cauliflower-Curry Soup

## Serves 4

Salt
1 large head cauliflower, cut into florets (5–6 cups)
1 tablespoon unsalted butter
1 medium onion, chopped
1 celery stalk, chopped
1 teaspoon curry powder
6 cups chicken stock
1 cup heavy cream
Freshly ground pepper
Extra-virgin olive oil, for serving

For years cauliflower was exiled to the back corner of the crudité platter. It's time to make the wonderfulness of the vegetable en vogue again.

This is a fantastic soup. You can keep it for days in the fridge, and it will get better and better—if it lasts that long!

**1.** Bring a large saucepan of salted water to a boil.

**2.** Add the cauliflower and cook until soft, 12 to 15 minutes. Drain and set aside.

**3.** Melt the butter in another large saucepan over medium-high heat. Cook the onion and celery, stirring, until soft, 3 to 4 minutes. Stir in the curry powder.

**4.** Add the cauliflower and stock and bring to a boil. Reduce the heat to low and simmer for 5 minutes.

**5.** Use an immersion blender to puree the soup until smooth and creamy, or transfer to a regular blender, puree, and return to the saucepan.

**6.** Add the cream, simmer for 2 minutes, and season with salt and pepper.

**7.** Pour into bowls and serve, drizzled with a little olive oil.

# Chinese Noodle Soup

**Serves 4**

Salt
8 cups chicken stock
2 boneless, skinless chicken
   breasts (about 1 pound)
8 ounces dried Chinese rice
   noodles
3 baby bok choy, leaves broken
   apart
1 cup thinly sliced red cabbage
1 scallion, thinly sliced
4 soft-boiled eggs, peeled and cut
   in half
Hot sauce

I make this soup whenever I start to feel under the weather. It's best prepared with good chicken stock. I put in a soft-boiled egg and a few splashes of hot sauce at the end to make sure that my nasty cold gets kicked to the curb.

**1.** Bring a large saucepan of salted water to a boil.

**2.** Meanwhile, bring the stock to a boil in another large saucepan.

**3.** Add the chicken to the stock and simmer until cooked through, about 18 minutes.

**4.** Add the noodles to the boiling water and cook, stirring occasionally, according to the package directions. Drain and divide the noodles among four bowls.

**5.** When the chicken is done, remove it from the stock and cut it into large cubes. Divide it among the bowls.

**6.** Divide the bok choy, cabbage, scallion, and eggs among the bowls.

**7.** Season with the hot sauce and serve.

# Bruschetta with Peas, Pancetta & Ricotta

## Serves 4

4 ounces pancetta, cubed
½ cup peas, fresh or frozen, thawed
  Salt
½ cup whole-milk ricotta
12 baguette slices, toasted
  Fresh basil leaves (torn if large)
  About 2 tablespoons
    extra-virgin olive oil
  Freshly ground pepper

I love making bruschetta and often try out new topping combinations on my partner and guests. Other possibilities are prosciutto and figs; blue cheese and nuts; cream cheese and roasted vegetables; and, for dessert, Nutella with baked strawberries.

**1.** Heat a skillet over medium heat and cook the pancetta until golden, about 4 minutes. Drain on paper towels. Set aside.

**2.** Have ready a bowl of ice water. In a small saucepan, cook the fresh peas in boiling salted water for 2 minutes, then dunk them into the ice water. Drain on paper towels. (If using frozen peas, cook for 30 seconds, rinse under cold water, and drain on paper towels.)

**3.** Spread a layer of ricotta on the baguette slices and top evenly with the pancetta, peas, and basil.

**4.** Drizzle with a little olive oil, sprinkle with some salt and pepper, and serve.

"Lemons are one of

my favorite ingredients."

# Roasted Asparagus & Tomato Salad with White Beans

## Serves 4

20 cherry tomatoes, cut in half
1 bunch asparagus, tough ends discarded
1 red chile pepper, cut in half, seeds removed
5 tablespoons olive oil
Salt and freshly ground pepper
1 (19-ounce) can cannellini beans, rinsed and drained
4 tablespoons extra-virgin olive oil
4 ounces herbal salad mix
1 tablespoon balsamic vinegar

Roasting gives new life to vegetables even when they are out of season, bringing out their sweetness. Combine roasted tomatoes and asparagus with some beans, and you have a salad that's perfect whatever the season.

**1.** Preheat the oven to 400°F.

**2.** Place the tomatoes, asparagus, and chile pepper on a baking sheet. Drizzle with 2 tablespoons of the oil and season with salt and pepper.

**3.** Roast until tender, about 5 minutes.

**4.** Meanwhile, put the beans and 1 tablespoon of the remaining oil in large skillet over medium heat and cook, stirring, until heated through, about 3 minutes.

**5.** Arrange the salad mix and white beans on a large platter. Cut the roasted chile into strips and place it on the salad with the rest of the vegetables.

**6.** Drizzle with the remaining 1 tablespoon oil and the balsamic vinegar, season with salt and pepper, and serve.

# Red Cabbage & Grapefruit Salad

## Serves 4

2 grapefruits
¼ red cabbage, finely shredded
1 cup crumbled fresh goat cheese
¼ cup pine nuts, toasted
2–4 tablespoons sherry vinegar
¼ cup extra-virgin olive oil
Salt and freshly ground pepper

Talk about color! Red cabbage has a pure jewel hue, and shredded finely, it's great in salads. If you put it in ice water, it becomes supercrisp and loses any bitterness. This salad is like a spa day on a plate, very healthy and supremely tasty.

**1.** Cut the peel off the grapefruits. Holding the grapefruits over a bowl to capture the juice, cut between each membrane to liberate the segments. Squeeze the membranes into the bowl to extract the rest of the juice.

**2.** Put the grapefruit segments, cabbage, cheese, and pine nuts in a serving bowl. Reserve the grapefruit juice.

**3.** In a small bowl, mix together ¼ cup of the reserved grapefruit juice, 2 tablespoons of the vinegar, and the oil. Taste the dressing and add more vinegar if desired.

**4.** Pour the dressing over the salad, season with salt and pepper, toss gently, and serve.

# Zucchini Salad with Goat Cheese

## Serves 4

7 tablespoons extra-virgin olive oil
1 large zucchini, thinly sliced
 lengthwise
 Salt and freshly ground pepper
5 ounces baby spinach
²/₃ cup walnuts, toasted
1 cup crumbled fresh goat cheese
2 tablespoons sherry vinegar

Squash complements many foods, and I like to pair it with a sour cheese like fresh goat cheese or feta. Sweet squash, tender spinach, tangy cheese, and crunchy nuts combine in this exemplary salad.

**1.** Heat 3 tablespoons of the oil in a large skillet and cook the zucchini slices, turning once, until golden, 2 to 3 minutes. Season with salt and pepper.

**2.** Combine the zucchini, spinach, walnuts, and goat cheese on a serving platter or in a serving bowl.

**3.** Sprinkle with salt and pepper, drizzle with the remaining 4 tablespoons oil and the sherry vinegar, and serve.

## "Keep Your Brain Alive, Paul!"

Wherever Mormor was, you would find a deck of cards. Playing solitaire was a passion and a compulsion. She would sit listening to jazz, drinking port, and playing solitaire for hours. Sometimes she would be sitting at the kitchen table playing cards when I went to bed and when I woke in the morning, she would be still sitting in the same spot. Only her new outfit told me that she had not been up all night playing.

When I was seven or eight, she bought me my own deck and taught me how to play. She would say, "Paul, this will keep your brain alive!"

To this day, I don't let a day go by without playing at least one game.

# Skagen Salad

## Serves 4

½ pound lump crabmeat (pick over and discard any shell pieces)
½ pound small shrimp or rock shrimp, peeled and cooked
¾ cup mayonnaise
¼ cup fresh lemon juice
2 tablespoons chopped fresh dill
1 small red onion, finely chopped
Salt and freshly ground pepper
Toast, for serving

Skagen is the name of a beach in the north of Denmark. Danish beaches don't have a Saint-Tropez feel, so I guess they had to compensate by inventing this absolutely wonderful seafood salad.

Danes, Swedes, and Norwegians all make this dish, often with crayfish. For years it was my mom's go-to appetizer, and she always served it in halved avocados. I usually serve it for lunch on toast or in a baked potato—or even on top of a burger for a very Scandinavian surf and turf.

**1.** In a medium bowl, mix together the crab, shrimp, mayonnaise, lemon juice, dill, and red onion. Season with salt and pepper.

**2.** Chill for 30 minutes in the fridge before serving to let the flavors blend.

**3.** Serve with toast.

# Kale Caesar!

Serves 4

½ cup plus 3 tablespoons
    extra-virgin olive oil
2 (6-ounce) boneless, skinless
    chicken breasts
    Salt and freshly ground
    pepper
5 slices good bread
8–10 Tuscan kale leaves
½ cup shaved Parmesan
2 tablespoons pine nuts,
    toasted
1 tablespoon Dijon mustard
1 teaspoon sherry vinegar
1 teaspoon finely chopped
    shallot

Caesar has always been my favorite Roman and my favorite salad. History books and PBS period dramas always make the ruler look chic. I've taken the Roman salute "Hail Caesar!" and made this salad in homage.

Nutritious and tasty kale stands in for the more pedestrian romaine lettuce. Toasted pine nuts add crunch, along with homemade croutons.

Be sure to cut out the tough stalks of the kale. I also find it best to give the leaves a gentle massage to loosen up the fibers, then place the kale in icy water to make it supercrisp.

**1.** Heat 1 tablespoon of the olive oil in a medium skillet over medium-high heat. Season the chicken with salt and pepper and sauté until cooked through, 5 to 6 minutes per side. Remove from the skillet and let rest while you make the salad.

**2.** Meanwhile, preheat the oven to 400°F, with a rack in the middle position.

**3.** Cut off the crusts of the bread and cut the bread into ½-inch-thick strips. Place it on a baking sheet, drizzle with 2 tablespoons of the oil, and bake until the croutons are golden, 3 to 4 minutes.

**4.** Cut off and discard the stems of the kale and cut the rest into thin strips. Gently massage the kale to break up the fibers a bit, then soak the leaves in a bowl of ice water.

**5.** Slice the chicken.

**6.** Dry the kale with paper towels and divide it among four bowls. Add the croutons, sliced chicken, Parmesan, and pine nuts. Season with salt and pepper.

**7.** In a jar or small bowl, shake or mix the remaining ½ cup oil, mustard, vinegar, and shallot until creamy. Season with salt and pepper.

**8.** Pour the dressing over the salad, toss, and serve.

# Quick Risotto with Asparagus

## Serves 4

- 4 tablespoons (½ stick) butter
- 1 medium onion, finely chopped
- 1 cup raw quick-cooking rice (such as Success)
- 5 cups chicken stock, warmed
- 10 asparagus stalks, tough ends discarded, cut into 2-inch pieces (about 1½ cups)
- 1 cup freshly grated Parmesan, plus more for serving
  Salt and freshly ground pepper
- 1 tablespoon finely chopped fresh parsley

I might get a mob of foodies mad at me for saying this, but you can make great risotto with quick rice. It cuts down on the cooking time and there's not nearly as much stirring. I have served this dish to unknowing dinner guests who pride themselves on their culinary expertise, and they have oohed and aahed over it.

This can be our little secret.

**1.** Melt 3 tablespoons of the butter in a large saucepan, add the onion, and cook, stirring, until soft, 3 to 4 minutes.

**2.** Add the rice and stir to coat it with the butter.

**3.** Add 1 cup of the stock and stir until it is absorbed, about 2 minutes. Stir in the asparagus.

**4.** Stir in more stock, about a cup at a time, stirring until the rice is al dente, about 10 minutes.

**5.** Stir in the remaining 1 tablespoon butter and the Parmesan and season with salt and pepper.

**6.** Serve with the parsley and extra Parmesan sprinkled on top.

# Pasta with Chunky Pesto

## Serves 4

Salt
2 cups fresh basil leaves
1 cup freshly grated Parmesan, plus more for serving
¼ cup pine nuts, toasted
1 garlic clove, chopped
½ cup extra-virgin olive oil
1 pound pasta (any kind)

I never make pesto in a blender or food processor. Chopping it by hand, then mixing in the oil and muddling it with a fork makes it both chunky and more flavorful. The process takes a little more time and elbow grease, but it's worth it.

This pesto is good on pasta or over chicken or pork or any white fish. You can even use it as a dip.

**1.** Bring a large pot of salted water to a boil.

**2.** Meanwhile, place the basil, Parmesan, pine nuts, and garlic on a cutting board and chop until all the ingredients are mingled together.

**3.** Transfer the pesto to a small bowl, add the olive oil, and mix well with a fork.

**4.** Add the pasta to the boiling water and cook, stirring occasionally, according to the package directions, until al dente. Drain.

**5.** Place the pasta in a large bowl, add the pesto, mix well, and serve immediately with extra Parmesan.

# Spaghetti Carbonara

## Serves 4

Salt
7 ounces bacon, cut into ½-inch dice
1 pound spaghetti
1 cup heavy cream
4 large egg yolks
2 cups freshly grated Parmesan, plus more for serving
½ cup frozen green peas, thawed
¼ teaspoon freshly ground pepper

With simple cooking, it's all about the ingredients. For my carbonara, I like to use farm-fresh eggs, which make this dish shine. Their yolks are a deep orange, versus the pale yellow of most grocery-store eggs. If you have a local egg farm or farmers' market, try fresh eggs for yourself. The peas add a nice hit of color.

**1.** Bring a large pot of salted water to a boil.

**2.** Meanwhile, heat a medium skillet over medium heat and cook the bacon until crispy, turning occasionally, 5 to 7 minutes. Drain on paper towels. Set aside.

**3.** Cook the spaghetti in the boiling water, stirring occasionally, according to the package directions, until al dente. Drain.

**4.** While the pasta is cooking, mix the cream, egg yolks, Parmesan, peas, ½ teaspoon salt, and the pepper in a large bowl.

**5.** Add the hot pasta to the cream mixture and toss well. Mix in the bacon and serve immediately with extra Parmesan.

# Fish Tacos with Salsa & Red Cabbage

## Serves 4

**Salsa**

- 20 heirloom cherry tomatoes, chopped
- ½ cup finely chopped red onion
- ½ red chile pepper, seeds removed and finely chopped
- 2 scallions, thinly sliced
- 3 tablespoons extra-virgin olive oil
  Salt and freshly ground pepper

**Tacos**

- 2 tablespoons butter
- 1½ pounds cod fillets or any other white fish
- 2 teaspoons chipotle chile powder
  Salt and freshly ground pepper
- 8 corn tortillas, heated in a warm pan
- 2 cups shredded red cabbage
- 1 lime, cut into wedges

True Mexican food is fresh, colorful, and bursting with flavor, nothing like most of what we get in America. It's clean and simple, yet refined. I fell in love with this taco at a shack on the beach near Playa del Carmen that served whatever fish the owner caught that morning. He grilled the fish and immediately placed it into simple tacos. ¡Qué rico!

With fresh cod, you can easily re-create this beach treat at home.

**1. To make the salsa:** Mix the tomatoes, onion, chile, scallions, and oil in a small bowl. Season with salt and pepper.

**2. To make the tacos:** Heat the butter in a medium skillet over medium heat. Season the fish with the chile powder, salt, and pepper.

**3.** Cook the fish for 3 to 4 minutes on each side, or until it is translucent and easily flaked.

**4.** Fill the tortillas with the fish, shredded red cabbage, and salsa, top with a squeeze of fresh lime juice, and serve.

# Fennel & Garlic Mussels

## Serves 4

- 4  pounds mussels
- 2  tablespoons butter
- 4  large shallots, thinly sliced
- 4  garlic cloves, finely chopped
- 1  small fennel bulb, thinly sliced
- 2  cups dry white wine
- ½  cup chopped mixed fresh parsley and dill

My family had a small cabin by the sea, and I loved hunting for mussels with my father at low tide. We would check the almanac to see when the tide was out, put on our Wellington boots, and bring a big galvanized steel bucket. The mussels were at their freshest, and after a good scrub and a little culinary magic from my mother, they ended up as lunch. The mild licorice flavor of fennel is an ideal complement to the sweet mussels. Serve with a spoon, so you can get all of the delicious broth.

**1.** Rinse and scrub the mussels in a large colander under cold running water. Discard any with cracked shells. Remove the beards.

**2.** Melt the butter in a large pot over medium-high heat. Add the shallots, garlic, and fennel and cook, stirring occasionally, until soft, about 5 minutes.

**3.** Add the mussels and wine to the pot, stir, and cover. Cook until they are all open, about 5 minutes. If there are any mussels that don't open, cook for a few minutes more. If they still don't open, discard them.

**4.** Stir in the herbs and serve.

# 4 from 1 Yeast Dough

## Basic Dough

1 tablespoon honey
1 envelope active dry yeast
1½ cups warm water (110°F)
3¾ cups unbleached all-purpose
   flour
1 teaspoon salt
2 tablespoons extra-virgin olive oil

**1.** Combine the honey, yeast, and water in the bowl of a stand mixer or in a large bowl. Let stand for 5 minutes, or until bubbly. (If it does not form bubbles, start over with new yeast.)

**2.** Add the rest of the ingredients and mix well in the mixer or with a wooden spoon.

**3.** Knead the dough for about 5 minutes in the mixer or turn it out onto a lightly floured work surface and knead for 10 minutes by hand.

**4.** Cover with plastic wrap and let rise for 1 hour in a warm place, or until doubled in size.

## Grissini

### Makes about 40 grissini

1 recipe Basic Dough (above)

**1.** Preheat the oven to 400°F, with racks in the upper and lower thirds. Line two baking sheets with parchment paper.

**2.** Divide the dough into 40 equal pieces.

**3.** Roll each piece out into a thin sausage 13 to 14 inches long. Place on the baking sheets, 2 inches apart.

**4.** Bake for 5 to 6 minutes, or until golden, rotating the pans from top to bottom and front to back at the halfway mark.

**5.** Cool on a wire rack and serve warm.

## Dinner Rolls

### Makes 10 rolls

1 recipe Basic Dough (above)
 Water
 Coarse sea salt

**1.** Preheat the oven to 375°F, with a rack in the middle position. Line a baking sheet with parchment paper.

**2.** Divide the dough into 10 equal pieces. Roll them into balls. Place on the baking sheet; it's OK if they touch.

**3.** Use scissors or a sharp knife to cut a shallow X on top of each roll. Brush with a little water and sprinkle lightly with salt.

**4.** Bake until golden, 12 to 14 minutes.

**5.** Cool on a wire rack before serving.

# Pizza

Makes 4 individual 8- to 10-inch pizzas

1 recipe Basic Dough (page 144)
Sliced tomatoes
Grated cheese

**1.** Preheat the oven to 400°F, with racks in the lower and upper thirds. Line two baking sheets with parchment paper.

**2.** Divide the dough into 4 equal pieces. On a lightly floured surface, roll out each piece into an 8- to 10-inch circle.

**3.** Place the dough circles on the baking sheets and divide the toppings among them.

**4.** Bake until golden, about 15 minutes, rotating the pans from top to bottom and front to back at the halfway mark.

**5.** Serve hot or warm.

# Cinnamon Buns

Makes 12 buns

1 recipe Basic Dough (page 144)
6 tablespoons (¾ stick) unsalted butter, at room temperature
1 packed cup light brown sugar
1 tablespoon ground cinnamon
1 cup almond slivers, toasted

**1.** Preheat the oven to 375°F, with a rack in the middle position. Line a baking sheet with parchment paper.

**2.** Roll the dough on a lightly floured surface into a 13-x-19-inch rectangle.

**3.** Mix the butter, brown sugar, and cinnamon in a small bowl.

**4.** Spread the butter mixture all over the dough with your fingers and sprinkle evenly with the almonds.

**5.** Roll up the dough along a long side into a log. Cut crosswise into 12 equal slices and place on the baking sheet, 2 inches apart.

**6.** Cover with plastic wrap and let rise for 30 minutes in a warm place.

**7.** Bake for 18 to 20 minutes, or until golden.

**8.** Cool on a wire rack before serving, if you can wait that long!

"Life is too short for boring food." — Paul Lowe

# Nutty Berry Crumble

1   cup blueberries
1   cup raspberries
1   cup blackberries
¼   cup granulated sugar
¼   cup plus 1 tablespoon
    unbleached all-purpose flour
1   cup mixed chopped nuts (I use
    walnuts, pecans, and almonds
    with skins)
¼   packed cup light brown sugar
½   teaspoon salt
3   tablespoons butter

You can, of course, use any fruit or berries you like. Make the crumble with one kind of berry (you could even use thawed frozen) or berries mixed with peaches or nectarines or plums. In the fall, try diced apples or pears.

**1.** Preheat the oven to 375°F, with a rack in the middle position.

**2.** In a small baking dish (about 1½ quarts), toss the berries with the granulated sugar and 1 tablespoon of the flour.

**3.** Mix the nuts, the remaining ¼ cup flour, the brown sugar, salt, and butter with your hands in a small bowl until thoroughly combined. Place the mixture on top of the berries.

**4.** Bake until golden and bubbly, about 20 minutes.

**5.** Cool slightly and serve.

# Chocolate & Raspberry Cake

## Serves 8 to 10

16  tablespoons (2 sticks) butter, at room temperature, plus more for the pan
1⅓  packed cups light brown sugar
3  large eggs, at room temperature
2  cups unbleached all-purpose flour
1  teaspoon baking powder
⅓  cup unsweetened cocoa powder
½  teaspoon salt
1  cup sour cream
9  ounces bittersweet chocolate, melted
1½  cups fresh raspberries

To my palate, nothing pairs as well with chocolate as raspberries. In this recipe, bittersweet meets cocoa powder. Mormor used to make a version of this cake, but she crushed the berries, whereas I leave them whole because I love the way whole berries sink slightly into the cake while it bakes, creating pockets of intense flavor.

**1.** Preheat the oven to 350°F, with a rack in the middle position. Butter a 9-inch springform pan.

**2.** In the bowl of a stand mixer fitted with the paddle attachment or in a large bowl with an electric mixer, beat the butter and brown sugar on high speed until creamy, 2 to 3 minutes. Beat in the eggs, one at a time.

**3.** Add the flour, baking powder, cocoa, and salt and mix well.

**4.** Mix in the sour cream and melted chocolate until the batter is smooth.

**5.** Scrape the batter into the springform pan and sprinkle it with the raspberries.

**6.** Bake for 55 to 60 minutes, or until set. A cake tester should come out wet but the center of the cake should stay still when you jiggle the pan. Don't overbake, or the cake will be dry.

**7.** Cool completely on a wire rack. Run a knife around the edge of cake, remove the sides of the pan, and serve.

# Orange & Hazelnut Cake

Serves 10

8 tablespoons (1 stick) butter, at room temperature, plus more for the pan
1 large orange
2 cups granulated sugar
5 large eggs, at room temperature
2 cups hazelnut flour (see headnote)
½ cup unbleached all-purpose flour
2 teaspoons baking powder
½ teaspoon salt
½ cup orange juice
½ cup water
 Seeds from ½ vanilla bean

This special cake is incredibly moist, with hazelnut flour imparting a sophisticated edge. It bursts with orange flavor thanks to a whole orange that's simmered until soft and then pureed. The orange-vanilla syrup that's poured over the cake before serving takes this cake over the top.

You can find hazelnut flour in many good supermarkets or health food stores or online. You can also substitute almond flour. For the orange, use a navel, Cara Cara, or blood orange.

**1.** Preheat the oven to 350°F, with a rack in the middle position. Thoroughly butter a Bundt pan.

**2.** Put enough water in a medium saucepan to cover the orange, bring to a boil, and boil for 10 to 15 minutes, or until the orange is soft. Cool slightly, then cut the orange in half and discard the seeds. Puree in a food processor, measure out 1 cup of the puree, and set aside.

**3.** In the bowl of a stand mixer fitted with the paddle attachment or in a large bowl with an electric mixer, beat the butter and 1 cup of the sugar on high speed until light and creamy, 2 to 3 minutes. Beat in the eggs, one at a time. Beat in the pureed orange.

**4.** Mix in the hazelnut flour, all-purpose flour, baking powder, and salt.

**5.** Scrape the batter into the Bundt pan and bake for about 40 minutes, or until a toothpick inserted into the cake comes out clean.

**6.** Cool on a wire rack.

**7.** Run a knife around the sides of the cake and turn it out onto a serving platter.

**8.** Bring the orange juice, water, vanilla seeds, and the remaining 1 cup sugar to a boil in a small saucepan. Reduce the heat to low and simmer until syrupy, about 10 minutes.

**9.** Cool the syrup and pour it over the cake just before serving.

# Roasted Plum Bellinis

## Serves 4

2  ripe plums, halved and pitted
4  teaspoons light brown sugar
   Ice-cold sparkling wine

Sugar-roasted plums turn the cheapest sparkling wine into a delicious libation. There is no reason to use Champagne for this. (This is the only time you will hear me say those words.)

**1.** Preheat the oven to 400°F, with a rack in the middle position.

**2.** Place the plums skin side down on a baking sheet and sprinkle them with the sugar.

**3.** Bake until the plums are softened and start to get some color, about 10 minutes.

**4.** Puree the roasted plums in a food processor or blender. Cool completely.

**5.** Divide the plum puree among four Champagne flutes. Top with the sparkling wine and serve.

LESTAT SAYS HELLO!

WOOF
woof

My dog, Lestat, came into my life four years ago when I met my partner, Anthony. It was love at first sight, twice. I remember the first time I saw the pup. Anthony opened the door, and Lestat ran to us. I thought he looked like a cross between a stuffed animal and a bat, but Lestat is a purebred French Bulldog.

He hates the rain, loves his chew toys, and if it's cold, he refuses to go outside without his mohair sweater—and, of course, his Louis Vuitton leash. I've never met a more loving and trusting dog. He never leaves my side. When I cook, he's there with me—maybe not so much out of love as the hope that he'll catch some dropped morsels. ♥

# Lestat's Turkey Woof Balls

1 pound ground turkey
1 cup cooked brown rice (from
½ cup raw)
½ cup coarsely chopped cooked
broccoli
2 tablespoons coarsely chopped
fresh parsley
Vegetable oil for frying

I have a roster of dog recipes that I developed for Lestat, and I try to cook for him as often as I can. It's really not much trouble to make fresh food for your dog from inexpensive but high-quality ingredients. And believe me, your pets will consider it an extraspecial treat.

These turkey balls are Lestat's favorite, paws-down. I cook them in batches and freeze them so I can add one or two to his dry food a couple of times a week. I sometimes make a double batch and reserve half of the mix for myself. Then I add some grated ginger and garlic, season with spices, salt, and pepper, and serve the meatballs with pasta.

**1.** Place the ground turkey, rice, broccoli, and parsley in a medium bowl and mix well.

**2.** Roll the turkey mixture into walnut-sized balls.

**3.** Heat the oil in a large skillet over medium heat and fry the meatballs, turning, until golden on all sides, 6 to 7 minutes.

**4.** Cool and freeze in batches. The meatballs can be frozen for up to 2 months.

NOON

*make*

# Oyster-Shell Place Cards

## YOU WILL NEED:

Paper
Scissors
Pen
Sticks (I used white paper candy
    sticks)
Paper glue
Clean, dry oyster shells
Hot glue gun
Hot glue sticks

You don't need fishing nets and driftwood to give your table a seaside feel. These little boats made from oyster shells will lend a subtle nautical air to your next seafood feast.

**1.** Cut out triangles of paper for the sails.

**2.** Write the guests' names on the sails.

**3.** Cut the sticks to an appropriate length (2 to 3 inches).

**4.** Glue the sails to the sticks with the paper glue.

**5.** Once the sails are dry, glue them to the center of the oyster shells using a dab of hot glue.

# Herb Wreath

## You Will Need:

One 14-inch moss wreath form
8–10 small clay pots in different
    sizes (I use 1.75-inch and
    2.5-inch pots)
Hot glue gun
Hot glue sticks
Potting soil
8–10 herb plants

This potted-herb wreath is both a decorative object and a working herb garden. Since the moss-covered form is made to get wet, you can immerse the whole wreath in the sink to water it. You can swap in clover, succulents, or small violets for the herbs, if you like. Moss wreaths are available in florist-supply stores, craft stores, or online.

**1.** Begin by gluing the pots to the moss form, using a large amount of hot glue to ensure a tight grip and alternating between the larger and smaller pots.

**2.** Once the pots are affixed to the form, put a little potting soil in each. Put in an herb plant and cover with enough potting soil to fill the pot.

**3.** Water the pots and display.

# Tart Tin Mirror

## You will need:

1 vintage tart pan rim (I used an
    8-inch pan rim)
Mirror (see headnote)
Glue (I used Duco Cement)

Placing a mirror inside a vintage tart tin transforms it from a baking pan to a treasure. You'll need to have the mirror cut to size at your local hardware or glass store. This piece can be used as decor or as a tray for salt and pepper on a festive tablescape.

1. Bring the rim of the pan and the mirror to your local hardware or glass store and have the mirror cut to fit.

2. Glue the mirror to the inside of the tart tin. Let it set for about 1 minute and you're done.

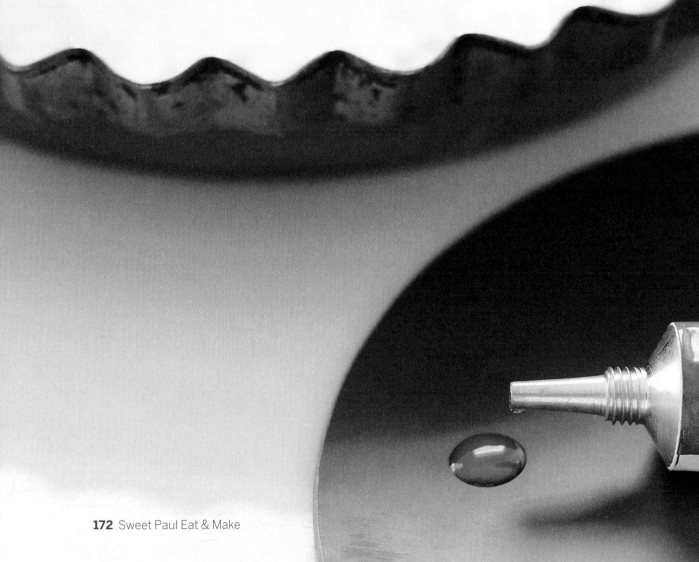

# Clothespin Trivet

## You will need:

40 spring-operated wooden
    clothespins
Dremel tool fitted with a drilling bit
    or a drill
Florist's wire

This trivet made of clothespins is a surefire conversation starter for your next afternoon tea.

**1.** Disassemble all 40 clothespins.

**2.** Using the Dremel tool, drill a small hole in each clothespin half about ½ inch from the tapered end.

**3.** Thread the clothespin pieces onto the wire in the same direction until they form a circle.

**4.** Once you have a full circle, wrap the ends of the wire together and twist until the clothespins are tight and secure.

"I LOVE T TRANSFORMING SOMETHING AS SIMPLE AS CLOTHESPINS INTO SOMETHING COOL AND MODERN." — PAUL LOWE

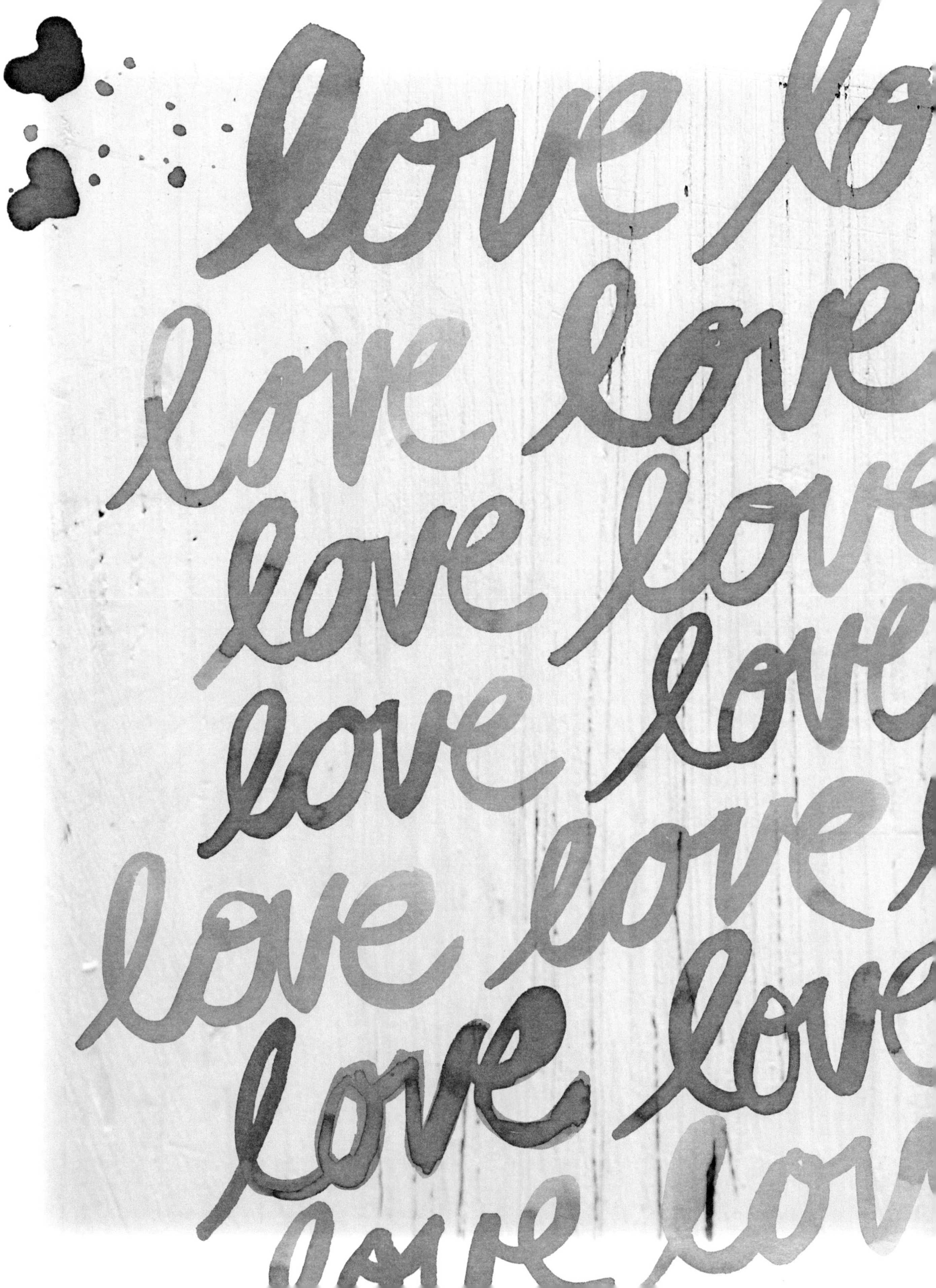

# Spice Bowls

I'm not a fan of spice shakers, since they make it hard to tell how much seasoning is added to a dish. For that reason, I keep salt and pepper and other frequently used dry seasonings in little spice bowls. The bowls add a sophisticated touch to the table. Little will your guests know that they are made from kids' modeling clay.

## YOU WILL NEED:

Rolling pin
Air-dry clay or polymer clay (I use
      Crayola Air-Dry Clay)
Coarse linen
Round biscuit cutter or drinking
      glass
Food-safe paint
Paint brush

**1.** Roll out the clay on the coarse linen to a thickness of ⅛ inch.

**2.** Using the biscuit cutter or a drinking glass, cut out circles of clay.

**3.** Form the disks into concave bowl shapes with your fingers.

**4.** Let dry or bake according to the manufacturer's instructions.

**5.** Paint the dried dishes. To clean, simply wipe them off.

# Vintage-Photo Napkins

Scanner
Old photos
Printable iron-on transfer paper
    (I use Lazertran)
Printer
Scissors (optional)
Iron
Ironing Board
Napkins (I use light linen ones)

With printable iron-on transfer paper, you can quickly turn napkins from mundane to special. I started with photos found at a flea market, but there are many other possibilities. Iron on pictures of a bride and groom and use the napkins for favors at a wedding. Get shots of your guests for a special dinner party and the napkins can become place cards. Or pull out old family photos and pay homage to your past.

**1.** Scan the photos.

**2.** Print them out onto transfer paper. (I like to cut around the edge of the subject before I transfer it.)

**3.** Iron the images onto napkins accordaing to the manufacturer's instructions.

**4.** Peel off the transfer paper and the napkins are ready.

# Punch Bowl Pendant Lamp

## You will need:

Dremel tool with a drilling or
   cutting bit
Plastic punch bowl
Spray paint (I use Liquitex)
Socket, cord, and plug from a
   lighting store
Screwdriver
Large wooden beads (optional
   decoration)
Scissors
Lightbulb
1 ceiling hook

This project was inspired by the cut-crystal lamp shades in my friend's Victorian brownstone. You can make your own lamp for just a few dollars with a plastic punch bowl from a party store and some spray paint. I like creamy white, but you can try a bold color if you prefer. If you tire of the look, buy another bowl and paint it a different color.

**1.** Use the Dremel tool to bore a ½-inch-diameter hole in the center of the bottom of the punch bowl.

**2.** Spray-paint the inside of the punch bowl and let dry.

**3.** Attach the light socket to the cord with the screwdriver according to the manufacturer's instructions.

**4.** Snake the cord through the hole in the punch bowl. (I add 2 wooden beads to the cord for decoration, but they're not necessary.)

**5.** Trim the cord to the desired length with the scissors and attach the plug to the other end of the cord.

**6.** Hang the pendant lamp.

**7.** Screw in a bulb and you're all set.

# Olive Oil Scrub

**YOU WILL NEED:**

3 tablespoons olive oil
3 tablespoons honey (I use organic)
½ cup granulated sugar

This three-ingredient facial scrub is a sweet and natural way to wash away a hard day in the kitchen.

**1.** Combine the ingredients in a jar or bowl and stir.

**2.** Gently massage the scrub into your skin in a circular motion and then rinse with warm water and pat dry with a soft towel.

"Kinda a clean hand freak: this scrub will make them shine." — Paul Lowe

# Washi-Tape Straws

**You will need:**

Paper straws
Washi tape
Scissors

Paper washi tape comes in a rainbow of colors and patterns and turns things from drab to fab in seconds. Using it, you can customize your straws for any occasion.

1. Apply washi tape to each straw in a spiral.

2. Trim off any excess tape from the end of the straws.

# NIGHT EAT + MAKE

On a midsummer evening when I was about five years old, Mormor, Auntie Gunnvor, and I were sitting on the porch when a craving struck me. There was only one thing to do: sneak into the house and raid Mormor's secret stash of cookies.

But when I reached the kitchen, I realized my plans were going to be more difficult to execute than I had thought, since the cookie jar was perched on top of the highest shelf. I pushed a chair to the counter and began to scale the cupboards to reach my prize. After all, what could go wrong?

CRASH! I fell to the floor and bit my lip terribly on the way down. Blood was everywhere, and I was sobbing. Mormor and Auntie Gunnvor dashed inside, picked me up off the floor, and rushed me to the emergency room. I needed two stitches, and for that, I'd need to have a needle in my lip. I screamed and cried and clamped my mouth shut. Mormor tried to bribe me to open it with toys and candy, to no avail. Finally, in desperation, she asked me what would make me calm down so that the doctors could stitch me up.

I immediately composed myself and replied, "I'd like fish pie, please."

I probably should have asked for a Louis Vuitton travel set, but even at that age, I knew that wonderful food cooked with love was the only remedy to make things better when they weren't going my way. The very next day Mormor took me into the kitchen and taught me to make her famous pie. Now whenever I feel down, I make it, and life is good again.

Mormor's Aquavit-Cured Salmon with Mustard Sauce

1 large piece skin-on wild salmon fillet cut from the head end of the fish, (about 1½ pounds)
1 large bunch fresh dill, chopped (about 1½ cups)
¼ cup kosher salt
¼ cup granulated sugar
2 tablespoons crushed pink peppercorns
Grated zest of 1 lemon
¼ cup aquavit
Mustard Sauce (recipe follows)

Every year for the holidays, Mormor would make her famous gravlax. It wouldn't have been Christmas without it. She would buy whole wild salmon at the market and fillet them herself, and the house would smell of fresh dill while she worked. Her secret was the addition of aquavit. I've added lemon zest for zing and pink peppercorns for a bit of heat and visual appeal. After your salmon is cured, slice it paper-thin and serve it on dark bread with mustard sauce. You can use cognac in place of the aquavit. You will need to start this 3 days in advance of serving.

**1.** Cut the salmon fillet in half crosswise.

**2.** Place one piece of fish skin side down in a glass dish large enough to hold it.

**3.** Mix the dill, salt, sugar, pink peppercorns, and lemon zest in a small bowl. Drizzle the aquavit over the salmon in the dish, then rub it with the salt mixture.

**4.** Top with the other piece of fish, skin side up. Cover with plastic wrap first, placed directly on the fish, then cover with foil.

**5.** Place a small cutting board on top of the fish and weigh it down with something heavy (I use tomato cans).

**6.** Refrigerate the salmon for 3 days, taking it out of the foil and plastic every 12 hours, basting it with the accumulated juices, and returning it to the setup and the refrigerator.

**7.** Discard the marinade. Scrape away the dill and any excess seasoning remaining on the fish. Slice the fish thinly on the diagonal and serve with the Mustard Sauce.

# MUSTARD SAUCE

MAKES 1 CUP

3 tablespoons extrastrong Dijon mustard (I use Maille)
1 tablespoon granulated sugar
1 tablespoon white wine vinegar
Salt and freshly ground pepper
¾ cup vegetable oil
2 tablespoons finely chopped fresh dill

No Norwegian would ever have gravlax without this sauce. Sometimes I'll make it with sweet mustard and serve it with cold cuts and cheese.

**1.** Mix the mustard, sugar, vinegar, and salt and pepper to taste in a small bowl.

**2.** Whisk in the oil, a few drops first, then in a thin stream, until the sauce is thickened.

**3.** Stir in the dill and serve. The sauce will keep for up to 1 week, refrigerated in an airtight container.

# French Onion Soup

## Serves 4

- 2 tablespoons butter
- 2 large onions, sliced (about 6 cups)
- 1 small red onion, sliced (about 1 cup)
- 4 garlic cloves, chopped
- 1 tablespoon unbleached all-purpose flour
- ½ cup dry white wine
- 6 cups beef stock
  Salt and freshly ground pepper
- 4 thick slices brioche or white bread
- 2 cups shredded Gruyère

I was twelve and in Paris with my parents when I first had French onion soup. We stayed in a small hotel in the 7th arrondissement near the Eiffel Tower, and my mom bought me a pair of beige corduroys, a brown blazer, and brown lace-up suede shoes. I felt like a Parisian.

One night we went to a tiny restaurant that served only two things: onion soup and beef entrecôte. The onion soup was the best thing I had ever tasted—sweet caramelized onions, a hearty broth, and Gruyère cheese.

If you make onion soup with single slices of bread, they sink and get soggy, but toasted cubes stay on top and keep crispy. I add a small red onion for additional sweetness, and some white wine for a little acidity.

**1.** Melt the butter in a large saucepan over medium heat. Add the onions and garlic and sauté until they are soft and translucent, about 15 minutes.

**2.** Stir in the flour and the wine. Stir in the stock, bring to a simmer, reduce the heat to low, and simmer for 30 minutes. Season with salt and pepper.

**3.** Preheat the oven to broil on high, with a rack in the upper third.

**4.** Cube the bread, place on a baking sheet, and toast in the oven until golden, about 2 minutes, tossing once.

**5.** Pour the soup into four ovenproof bowls, top with the bread, and cover with the cheese.

**6.** Broil until the cheese is melted, about 3 minutes.

**7.** Serve steaming hot.

# CREAMY POLENTA WITH KALE & MUSHROOMS

## SERVES 4

5 cups water
1 cup polenta or cornmeal
¼ cup freshly grated Parmesan
3 tablespoons heavy cream
2 tablespoons butter
  Salt and freshly ground pepper
2 tablespoons extra-virgin olive
  oil, plus more for serving
2 pounds mixed mushrooms
  (whatever kinds you like best),
  cut in half
2 shallots, finely chopped
1 bunch kale (8 large leaves),
  shredded
  Sherry vinegar, for serving

I didn't know about polenta until I came to the United States, but I was an instant convert. You do need to babysit polenta while it cooks so you get the ideal creamy texture, but it's worth it. Here I top it with mushrooms and kale (something else I hadn't encountered in Norway), but you can also top it with ragu sauce (page 198) if you're in the mood for something meaty.

**1.** Bring the water to a boil in a large saucepan.

**2.** Gradually add the polenta, whisking all the while.

**3.** Reduce the heat to medium and cook until thickened, stirring frequently, about 30 minutes.

**4.** Remove from the heat. Stir in the cheese, cream, and butter. Season with salt and pepper, cover, and keep warm.

**5.** Heat the oil in a large skillet over medium-high heat, add the mushrooms and shallots, and cook, stirring, until the shallots are golden, 8 to 10 minutes.

**6.** Add the kale and cook until the kale starts to soften, about 2 minutes. Season with salt and pepper.

**7.** Divide the polenta among four bowls and top with the kale mixture.

**8.** Drizzle with a little sherry vinegar and olive oil and serve.

# ROASTED VEGETABLE SHEPHERD'S PIE

## SERVES 4

- 3 medium tomatoes, diced
- 1 medium zucchini, diced (about 1 cup)
- 1 small eggplant, diced (about 2 cups)
- 1 large onion, diced
- 1 yellow bell pepper, cored, seeded, and diced
- 1 red bell pepper, cored, seeded, and diced
- 2 garlic cloves, thinly sliced
- 3 tablespoons extra-virgin olive oil
  Salt and freshly ground pepper
- 1 teaspoon chopped fresh rosemary
- 5 large Idaho potatoes, peeled and cubed
- ½ cup whole milk, warmed
- 2 tablespoons butter

I created this crowd-pleasing dish especially for one of my vegetarian friends. Zucchini, eggplant, sweet bell peppers, and tomatoes are roasted to make something similar to ratatouille. The vegetables are then topped with mashed potatoes. Rosemary provides a hint of earthiness. It can serve as a hearty meal or a side to beef or roast chicken.

**1.** Preheat the oven to 400°F, with a rack in the middle position.

**2.** Place the tomatoes, zucchini, eggplant, onion, bell peppers, and garlic on a rimmed baking sheet. Drizzle with the oil and season with salt, pepper, and the rosemary.

**3.** Bake until the vegetables start to soften, 18 to 20 minutes.

**4.** Place the vegetables in a 2½-quart baking dish and keep warm.

**5.** Preheat the broiler.

**6.** Meanwhile, place the potatoes in a pot of unsalted water and bring to a boil.

**7.** Boil until soft, 15 to 20 minutes. Drain the potatoes and return them to the pot. Add the milk and butter and mash with a potato masher until creamy. Season with salt and pepper.

**8.** Spread the mashed potatoes over the vegetables, using the back of a spoon to give the potatoes some texture.

**9.** Broil until the potatoes are golden, with the tips browned. Watch carefully, so they don't burn.

**10.** Serve hot.

# Pasta with Roasted Butternut Squash, Garlic & Lemon

Salt
½ medium butternut squash, peeled, seeded, and cut into ½-inch pieces (about 3 cups)
6 garlic cloves, cut in half
1 sprig fresh rosemary
¼ cup plus 3 tablespoons extra-virgin olive oil
Freshly ground pepper
1 pound spaghetti
Grated zest of 1 lemon
¼ cup fresh lemon juice
2 tablespoons drained nonpareil capers
1 cup freshly grated Parmesan
Fresh parsley leaves

Nothing beats a good pasta dish: It's easy and tasty and everybody loves it. I like my pasta relatively unadorned—no marinara sauce for me. I'm perfectly happy with some Parmesan, good oil, and fresh basil.

But when I want something a bit fancier, I make this butternut squash pasta, which holds true to my simple-with-good-ingredients rule. Salty capers and pungent rosemary offset sweet chunks of butternut squash. Toss with pasta and Parmesan, garnish with whole leaves of parsley, and you have a dish to satisfy the most discriminating palate.

**1.** Preheat the oven to 400°F, with a rack in the middle position.

**2.** Meanwhile, bring a large pot of salted water to a boil.

**3.** Place the butternut squash, garlic, and rosemary on a baking sheet and drizzle with 3 tablespoons of the oil. Sprinkle with salt and pepper.

**4.** Roast until golden and tender, turning once, about 15 minutes.

**5.** Add the spaghetti to the boiling water and cook it according to the package directions, until al dente.

**6.** Drain the spaghetti and place it in a large bowl.

**7.** Add the remaining ¼ cup oil, the lemon zest and juice, capers, Parmesan, and roasted vegetable mixture. Sprinkle with the parsley, toss, and serve.

SPICE. SPICE. SPICE. SPICE. SPICE. SPICE.

# Mac & Cheese

## Serves 6

3 tablespoons butter, plus
   2 tablespoons butter, melted
3 tablespoons unbleached
   all-purpose flour
3 cups whole milk, heated
¼ cup heavy cream
1 cup grated Gruyère
½ cup grated Jarlsberg
½ cup grated Monterey Jack
   Salt and freshly ground pepper
2 tablespoons extra-virgin olive oil
2 medium zucchini, sliced
1 pound pasta (I like to use shells)
1 cup cubed brioche, challah, or
   other good white bread

One of my favorite American dishes is mac and cheese. After living here for a while, I started playing with the recipe, and of course I had to incorporate Jarlsberg. I also like to balance the dish a little bit by adding some vegetables: Zucchini works well. Cubed bread rather than bread crumbs adds crunch to this gooey, decadent delight.

**1.** Preheat the oven to 425°F, with a rack in the middle position.

**2.** Meanwhile, bring a large pot of salted water to a boil.

**3.** Melt the 3 tablespoons butter in a large saucepan over medium heat, then whisk in the flour.

**4.** Whisk in the milk a little at a time, to prevent lumps.

**5.** Add the cream, bring to a simmer, and cook for 5 minutes, stirring constantly.

**6.** Stir in the cheeses and season with salt and pepper.

**7.** In a large skillet, heat the oil over medium heat and cook the zucchini, stirring, until golden, 4 to 5 minutes.

**8.** Meanwhile, cook the pasta in the boiling water according to the package instructions, until al dente, and drain.

**9.** Add the pasta and zucchini to the sauce and mix well.

**10.** Pour the mixture into a 9-x-13-inch baking dish.

**11.** Mix the bread cubes and the 2 tablespoons melted butter in a bowl and top the mac and cheese with the mixture.

**12.** Bake until the cheese is bubbly and the bread is golden, 10 to 12 minutes. Serve.

# Ragu Lasagna

## Serves 6

**Ragu Sauce**

- 2 tablespoons extra-virgin olive oil
- 1 celery stalk, finely chopped (about ½ cup)
- 1 large carrot, peeled and finely chopped (about 1 cup)
- 1 medium onion, finely chopped (about 1 cup)
- 2 garlic cloves, finely chopped
- ½ pound ground beef
- ½ pound ground pork or veal
- ½ pound bacon, finely diced
- 2 cups beef stock
- 1 cup dry red wine
- ½ cup tomato paste
- ½ cup whole milk
  Salt and freshly ground pepper

**Béchamel Sauce**

- 3 tablespoons butter
- ¼ cup unbleached all-purpose flour
- 1⅓ cups whole milk, warmed

- 9–12 lasagna noodles, cooked according to the instructions on the box
- 2 cups freshly grated Parmesan

This is one of the best of my never-fail dishes. I tasted a similar lasagna on a shoot for a food magazine years ago. Then I tinkered with the recipe in my kitchen for weeks to "Sweet Paulify" it, simplifying the ingredients and intensifying the flavors of the thick, meaty, red wine–based sauce. Parmesan is the only cheese. This is a hearty lasagna (the best kind) and it takes work, but the results make the effort worth it. If you like, use all ground beef for the sauce.

**1. To make the ragu sauce:** Heat the oil in a large saucepan. Add the celery, carrot, onion, and garlic and cook, stirring, for 3 minutes.

**2.** Add the meat and bacon and cook, stirring, until the meat is crumbly and no longer pink.

**3.** Stir in the stock, wine, tomato paste, and milk. Season with salt and pepper. Simmer until the ragu starts to thicken, about 30 minutes.

**4.** Preheat the oven to 375°F, with a rack in the middle position.

**5. Meanwhile, make the béchamel sauce:** Melt the butter in a medium saucepan, then whisk in the flour.

**6.** Whisk in the hot milk a little at a time, to prevent lumps. Cook until thickened, stirring constantly, about 2 minutes.

**7.** In a 9-x-13-inch baking dish, make a layer of one third of the ragu sauce, one quarter of the béchamel, and one quarter of the cheese. Top with 3 or 4 noodles. Make 2 more layers in the same way. Top with the remaining béchamel and Parmesan.

**8.** Cover with foil and bake for 40 minutes. Remove the foil and bake for 10 minutes more, until golden and bubbly.

**9.** Let stand for 15 minutes before serving.

# Mormor's Fish Pie

Salt
2 pounds cod fillets or other thick
white fish
3 tablespoons butter, plus
2 tablespoons, melted
¼ cup unbleached all-purpose flour
1⅓ cups whole milk, heated
3 large eggs
½ pound cooked peeled shrimp,
chopped
Pinch of freshly grated nutmeg
Freshly ground pepper
2 thick slices brioche or other
white bread, cut into 1-inch
cubes

Fish pie may sound like a pedestrian dish, but this combination of shrimp and cod napped with cream sauce and topped with cubes of crunchy brioche is sublime.

Mormor was famous in our neighborhood for her fish pie. My friends at school always wanted to come home with me just so they could taste it. She and Auntie Gunnvor got this recipe when they were children. Orphans from a very early age, they grew up in a home for girls. They had riveting stories about the trouble they got into. Many of their anecdotes involved sneaking into the kitchen for food. On one occasion, the cook caught them stealing a fish pie. Their punishment? The cook taught them the recipe, and they had to make several pies each week for a month for all the other girls in the orphanage. Their punishment is our reward.

**1.** Preheat the oven to 350°F, with a rack in the middle position.

**2.** Bring a large saucepan of salted water to a simmer, add the fish, and simmer until it flakes easily, 4 to 5 minutes.

**3.** Drain, flake the fish with a fork, and set aside.

**4.** Melt the 3 tablespoons butter in a saucepan, then whisk in the flour.

**5.** Whisk in the hot milk a little at a time, to prevent lumps. Remove from the heat and let cool.

**6.** Whisk in the eggs.

**7.** Gently stir in the fish and shrimp and season with the nutmeg and salt and pepper.

**8.** Place the fish mixture in a 10-inch pie plate.

**9.** Mix the bread cubes and the 2 tablespoons melted butter and distribute them on top of the pie.

**10.** Bake for 25 to 30 minutes, or until the pie is golden and set. Serve hot.

# Trout with Creamy Dill Sauce

**Sauce**
- 1 tablespoon butter
- 1 large shallot, finely chopped
- ½ cup dry white wine
- 1 cup heavy cream
- ½ cup bottled clam juice
- 1 tablespoon chopped fresh dill
- Salt and freshly ground pepper

- 4 (7-ounce) skin-on trout fillets
- Salt and freshly ground pepper
- 2 tablespoons butter
- 1 tablespoon chopped fresh dill

My mother loved to fish as much as she loved to eat it. Almost every fall, we would stay for a week in a mountain hotel, where the main activity was hours of fishing followed by luxurious fish dinners. I went with mixed feelings, since I've never been an outdoorsy guy. The only thing that could tear me from my spot in front of the fireplace with a good book was the dinner bell. This recipe was first given to my mother by the chef at the hotel, and she fixed it up a bit. I, in turn, have finessed it.

What sets the simple pan-fried trout apart is the sauce. Cream, dill, and trout create a perfect harmony. The clam juice is my addition for a hint of the sea.

**1. To make the sauce:** Melt the 1 tablespoon butter in a small saucepan over medium heat. Add the shallot and cook, stirring, until soft, about 3 minutes.

**2.** Add the wine and cook until reduced by half, about 3 minutes. Stir in the cream and clam juice and simmer until thickened, about 10 minutes.

**3.** Stir in the dill and season with salt and pepper. Keep warm.

**4.** Rub the fish with salt and pepper.

**5.** Melt the 2 tablespoons butter in a large skillet over high heat and fry the fish in batches for 2 minutes on each side, or until the flesh starts to flake.

**6.** Transfer the fish to a platter or plates, sprinkle with the dill, and serve with the sauce.

# Chicken with Olives & Capers

4 large or 8 small organic chicken
  thighs (about 2 pounds)
1 lemon, cut into wedges
1 cup mixed pitted olives
2 tablespoons drained nonpareil
  capers
  Juice of 1 lemon
2 tablespoons extra-virgin olive oil
  Salt and freshly ground pepper

This dish came about out of necessity, improvised with items I had on hand when some unexpected guests showed up. It was one of my best spontaneous dishes, and now I serve it regularly. The lemon juice tenderizes the chicken and the salty capers and olives mix with the juices to create a sauce.

You can use chicken thighs or buy a whole chicken and cut it into pieces.

**1.** Preheat the oven to 400°F, with a rack in the middle position.

**2.** Place the chicken skin side up in a baking dish. Scatter the lemon wedges, olives, and capers on top of the chicken.

**3.** Pour the lemon juice and olive oil over the chicken and sprinkle with salt and pepper.

**4.** Bake until golden, basting with the juices once, for 25 to 30 minutes, or until an instant-read thermometer inserted into the thickest part of a thigh reads 165°F. Serve.

# Maple-Roasted Chicken with Maple Gravy

## Serves 4

1 lemon, cut in half
1 whole organic chicken (about 3½ pounds)
¼ cup extra-virgin olive oil, plus more for rubbing the chicken
Salt and freshly ground pepper
15 small fingerling potatoes
4 shallots, cut in half
½ cup maple syrup
Maple Gravy (recipe follows)

This is my ultimate go-to dish, and it just about makes itself, all in one pan. The drippings are used to make the best gravy ever. It's so good that I could open up Sweet Paul's Gravy Joint. You're going to want to eat it by the spoonful. I always try to use organic chicken: You can taste the difference.

**1.** Preheat the oven to 400°F, with a rack in the middle position.

**2.** Place the lemon inside the cavity of the chicken. Tie the legs together with string.

**3.** Rub the chicken with olive oil and season it with salt and pepper. Place it in a roasting pan.

**4.** Add the potatoes and shallots.

**5.** Roast for 30 minutes. Pour the maple syrup and the ¼ cup olive oil over the chicken, then lower the oven temperature to 375°F.

**6.** Roast for 45 minutes longer. An instant-read thermometer inserted in a thigh should read 165°F and the juices should run clear. Reserve the drippings for the gravy.

**7.** Let the chicken rest for 10 minutes before cutting into pieces and serving it with the potatoes, shallots, and gravy.

# Maple Gravy

## Serves 4

1 tablespoon butter
1 shallot, finely chopped
½ cup chicken stock
½ cup drippings from Maple-Roasted Chicken (above), (skim fat first)
1½ cups heavy cream
1 teaspoon cornstarch, dissolved in 3 tablespoons cold water (optional)
Salt and freshly ground pepper

**1.** Melt the butter in a medium saucepan over medium heat. Add the shallots and cook, stirring, until soft, about 2 minutes.

**2.** Stir in the chicken stock and drippings and cook until reduced by half, about 5 minutes.

**3.** Stir in the cream and let the sauce simmer until thickened, about 30 minutes. If it is still not thick enough, stir in the cornstarch mixture.

**4.** Season with salt and pepper and serve hot with the chicken.

# Chorizo Burger

1 tablespoon extra-virgin olive oil
1 small red onion, chopped
1 pound ground beef
½ cup dried Spanish chorizo, finely
  chopped
½ teaspoon salt
¼ teaspoon freshly ground pepper
1 tablespoon vegetable oil
4 thick slices Gruyère cheese
4 brioche buns or other nice
  sandwich rolls
  Lettuce, tomato slices, and red
  onion slices

This is my take on a burger served at my local hangout, Building on Bond, in Brooklyn. I love the place, since they have great outdoor seating and I can take my dog, Lestat, with me when I drop by for lunch or a latte.

The secret behind the burger is the finely chopped chorizo mixed into the ground beef, which contributes spice, moisture, and texture. I love a thick slice of Gruyère on my burger, but you can use whatever cheese you want.

**1.** Heat the olive oil in a large skillet and cook the onion, stirring, until soft, 5 to 7 minutes. Cool.

**2.** Mix together the ground beef, chorizo, cooked onion, salt, and pepper in a medium bowl. Do not overwork.

**3.** Form the beef mixture into 4 patties.

**4.** Wipe out the skillet you cooked the onions in, add the vegetable oil, and cook the patties over medium-high heat for 3 to 4 minutes on each side for medium.

**5.** Place one slice of the cheese on each patty and let it melt.

**6.** Serve between the brioche buns with lettuce, tomato, and red onion.

# Norwegian Meatballs with Mashed Rutabaga

## Serves 4

1½ pounds ground beef
2 tablespoons unbleached
   all-purpose flour
   Salt and freshly ground pepper
¼ teaspoon ground ginger
   Pinch of freshly grated nutmeg
½ cup whole milk, plus 1 cup whole
   milk, warmed
1 large rutabaga, peeled and cut
   into cubes
4 tablespoons (½ stick) butter
   Brown Gravy (recipe follows)

Meatballs are very Scandinavian. I have no idea why: I must have been at home sick the day they taught us why the meatball is connected to our heritage. The Swedes have small meatballs that they serve with lingonberry jam and cream sauce, the Danes serve theirs with beet salad, and Norwegians have a larger version that we serve with mashed rutabaga, potatoes, and gravy. I'll let you in on a little secret: The Norwegian ones are the best!

This is my version of my mother's recipe.

**1.** Mix the beef, flour, 1½ teaspoons salt, ¼ teaspoon pepper, the ginger, and the nutmeg in a large bowl.

**2.** Add the milk and mix until the mixture is smooth.

**3.** Form into 8 large meatballs.

**4.** Place the rutabaga in a large saucepan of salted water, bring to a boil, and simmer until soft, about 15 minutes.

**5.** Meanwhile, melt 1 tablespoon of the butter in a large skillet over medium-high heat and brown the meatballs on all sides, about 4 minutes per side. Reduce the heat to low, cover, and cook until heated through, 5 to 8 minutes.

**6.** Drain the rutabaga and mash with the remaining 3 tablespoons butter and the 1 cup warmed milk. Season with salt and pepper.

**7.** Serve the meatballs with the mashed rutabaga and the gravy.

# Brown Gravy

## Serves 4

2 tablespoons butter
2 tablespoons unbleached
   all-purpose flour
1½–2 cups beef stock, warmed
   Salt and freshly ground
   pepper

**1.** Melt the butter in a medium saucepan over medium heat.

**2.** Add the flour and stir well.

**3.** Add the warm stock a little at a time and cook, stirring constantly with a whisk, until it gets nice and thick, about 5 minutes.

**4.** Season with salt and pepper and serve with the meatballs.

# Boeuf Bourguignon

## Serves 6

- 2 tablespoons butter
- 1 tablespoon extra-virgin olive oil
- 2 pounds beef chuck, cut into 1-inch cubes
  Salt and freshly ground pepper
- 2 medium carrots, peeled and chopped
- 10 shallots, cut in half
- 6 garlic cloves
- ½ cup diced pancetta
- 2 cups beef stock
- 1 (28-ounce) can diced tomatoes, drained
- 3 cups good dry red wine (about three fourths of a 750-ml bottle)
- 1 tablespoon tomato paste
- 1 bay leaf
- 15 black peppercorns, coarsely crushed
  Fresh parsley leaves

Julia Child is one of my greatest idols, and boeuf Bourguignon was one of the first recipes that I perfected. Not to brag, but my boeuf and I could take Julia and her boeuf any day.

I got the basic recipe from a butcher in a small town in Ile de Ré in France, who scrawled it in French on a piece of paper. I followed it as best as I could, and after some more testing, I made it foolproof.

Accompany with a green salad and some country-style bread.

**1.** Heat the butter and oil in a large heavy-bottomed saucepan or Dutch oven.

**2.** Sear the meat in batches on all sides. Season well with salt and pepper and set aside.

**3.** Add the carrots, shallots, garlic, and pancetta to the pan and cook, stirring, until the onions are softened, 6 to 7 minutes.

**4.** Add the stock, scraping up the browned bits from the bottom of the pot. Add the meat, diced tomatoes, red wine, tomato paste, bay leaf, and peppercorns.

**5.** Cover and let the stew simmer for 3 to 4 hours, or until the beef is tender, stirring every 15 minutes.

**6.** Skim the top of any fat. Sprinkle with the parsley and serve.

Red Wine– & Honey-Braised Short Ribs with Cauliflower Mash

1 teaspoon ground cumin
½ teaspoon ground coriander
2 garlic cloves, minced
1 teaspoon salt
¼ teaspoon freshly ground pepper
4 bone-in beef short ribs (about 1 pound each), cut into 8–12 pieces
1 tablespoon butter
1 large onion, finely chopped
1 celery stalk, finely chopped
2 cups dry red wine, plus more if needed
1 cup water
½ cup honey
¼ cup soy sauce
Cauliflower Mash (recipe follows)

There's nothing better than meat that's been braised in the oven for hours. This recipe for short ribs cooked until the meat is falling off the bone is never-fail, and the juices are truly heavenly. The onion and celery melt into the gravy, which is sweetened with honey, lightly salted from the soy sauce, and richly perfumed with cumin and coriander. Served it with mashed cauliflower or roasted potatoes that you should smush into the gravy.

**1.** Preheat the oven to 325°F, with a rack in the middle position.

**2.** Mix the spices with the garlic, salt, and pepper in a small bowl and rub them into the meat.

**3.** Melt the butter in a large Dutch oven over medium-high heat, add the ribs, and brown on all sides, in batches if necessary, 3 to 4 minutes per side. As they are browned, remove the ribs from the pan and set aside.

**4.** Add the onion and celery to the pan and cook, stirring, until soft, about 5 minutes.

**5.** Return the meat to the pan and add the wine, water, honey, and soy sauce. Bring to a boil.

**6.** Cover the pot with foil or a lid and bake until the meat easily falls off the bone, 2½ to 3 hours. Check after about 1 hour to make sure the liquid isn't bubbling too vigorously. If it is, lower the oven temperature to 300°F. Add more wine if the meat looks dry.

**7.** Skim the surface fat before serving.

**8.** Serve with the Cauliflower Mash.

# Cauliflower Mash

## Serves 4

Salt
1 large cauliflower, cut into florets
2 tablespoons butter
½–1 cup vegetable stock, warmed
Freshly ground pepper

I first had this dish at the home of my friend Frances Janisch, an übertalented photographer. It's so creamy that I had no idea it was cauliflower. It's a great way to cut back on carbs and calories without sacrificing flavor.

**1.** Bring a large saucepan of salted water to a boil, add the cauliflower, and cook until soft, 15 to 20 minutes. Drain and return to the pot.

**2.** Add the butter and ½ cup stock.

**3.** Mash with a potato masher. If the mash is too dry, add some more stock.

**4.** Season with salt and pepper and serve.

# Pork Roast Stuffed with Herbs & Garlic

## Serves 8

1 (7-pound) pork loin, boned
1 whole garlic head, peeled and finely chopped in a food processor
1 tablespoon finely chopped fresh parsley
1 tablespoon finely chopped fresh sage
1 tablespoon finely chopped fresh rosemary
  Salt and freshly ground pepper
2 tablespoons extra-virgin olive oil

I've never had the stamina or desire to tackle those recipes from gourmet magazines that seem to have pages of steps and prep. I like to be inspired and then simplify the dish without losing any flavor. This recipe, adapted from one my friend Ellen Silverman did for *Sweet Paul* a few years ago, doesn't break the bank or your back. There's no need to butterfly, pound, and tie a roast when it's so easy to poke a hole in it and push the stuffing in.

On the rare occasions that there are any leftovers, I love to thinly slice the pork and layer it on rye bread with sweet mustard.

**1.** Preheat the oven to 450°F, with a rack in the middle position.

**2.** Pat the pork loin dry. Using a knife-sharpening steel or a long-handled wooden spoon, pierce a hole lengthwise through the center of the loin.

**3.** Mix the garlic, herbs, 1 teaspoon salt, and ½ teaspoon pepper in a small bowl.

**4.** Working from both ends of the loin, use your fingers to stuff the garlic mixture into the hole.

**5.** Rub the olive oil all over the roast and season with more salt and pepper.

**6.** Place the loin in a shallow roasting pan and roast for 15 minutes. Reduce the oven temperature to 350°F and cook for 1¼ to 1½ hours more, turning the roast and basting it every 20 minutes with the juices. The roast is done when an instant-read thermometer inserted into the center registers 145°F.

**7.** Transfer the roast to a cutting board and let it rest for 15 minutes before carving and serving.

# Pork Tenderloin with Balsamic Raspberries

## Serves 4

- 2 pork tenderloins (about ¾ pound each), trimmed of excess fat
- 1 tablespoon extra-virgin olive oil
  Salt and freshly ground pepper
- 3 tablespoons butter
- 1 shallot, finely chopped
- 1 cup balsamic vinegar
- ¼ cup granulated sugar
- 2 cups fresh raspberries

Simmer shallots and inexpensive balsamic vinegar until syrupy, add some raspberries, and the result is a sauce at once sweet and tart. Pair it with pork tenderloin and you have an elegant entrée in 20 minutes.

**1.** Preheat the oven to 375°F, with a rack in the middle position.

**2.** Rub the meat with the oil and sprinkle it with salt and pepper.

**3.** Melt 2 tablespoons of the butter in a large skillet and brown the pork on all sides, 4 to 5 minutes.

**4.** Place the pork on a rack in a roasting pan and roast for 10 to 12 minutes; an instant-read thermometer inserted into the center should read 140°F.

**5.** Let the meat rest on a cutting board for 5 minutes.

**6.** Meanwhile, melt the remaining 1 tablespoon butter in a small saucepan over medium heat and cook the shallots, stirring, until soft, 2 to 3 minutes.

**7.** Stir in the balsamic vinegar, sugar, and ½ teaspoon salt and simmer until the sauce starts to thicken, about 10 minutes.

**8.** Season the sauce with pepper, add the raspberries, and heat just to warm.

**9.** Cut the meat into slices and serve with the warm balsamic raspberries.

# The Perfect Side Salad

## Serves 4

1 head lettuce (choose the kind you like the most)
1 cup walnuts, toasted
4 fresh figs, cut into quarters
1–2 cups shaved Parmesan
2 tablespoons extra-virgin olive oil
1 tablespoon sherry vinegar
Salt and freshly ground pepper

We all need a perfect little side salad, one that goes with anything from meat to fish to poultry and everything in between. This one does just that. The crunch of the walnuts and sweetness from the figs play against the saltiness of the Parmesan. I prefer to keep my dressings simple: some good olive oil, a splash of sherry vinegar, and, of course, salt and pepper.

**1.** Tear the lettuce into pieces and divide among four plates.

**2.** Add some of the walnuts, figs, and Parmesan to each.

**3.** Drizzle each salad with a little of the olive oil and sherry vinegar. Season with salt and pepper and serve.

4 FROM 1 YUKON GOLD POTATOES

# Truffle Mash

## Serves 4

3  pounds Yukon Gold potatoes, peeled
3  tablespoons butter
½  cup whole milk, warmed
   Salt and freshly ground pepper
1–2  teaspoons black truffle oil (available in gourmet stores)

**1.** Place the potatoes in a large saucepan of water. Bring to a boil and simmer until tender, about 10 minutes.

**2.** Drain, then return the potatoes to the pan.

**3.** Add the butter and milk and mash with a potato masher until smooth.

**4.** Season with salt and pepper, stir in truffle oil to taste, and serve.

# Hasselback Potatoes

## Serves 4

12  medium Yukon Gold potatoes
 2  tablespoons butter, melted
    Salt
 1  tablespoon paprika
12  bay leaves

**1.** Preheat the oven to 400°F, with a rack in the middle position.

**2.** Using a sharp knife, cut 8 slices almost three quarters of the way though each potato, leaving the bottom quarter intact and the slices still connected.

**3.** Place the potatoes on a baking sheet and brush with the butter, getting butter between all the slices.

**4.** Sprinkle with salt and paprika and place a bay leaf into each potato.

**5.** Bake until the potatoes are tender and cooked through, about 30 minutes.

**6.** Serve hot.

# Fried Smashed Potatoes

## Serves 4

20  small Yukon Gold potatoes
 2  tablespoons extra-virgin olive oil
    Vegetable oil for frying
    Salt
 2  tablespoons finely chopped fresh chives

**1.** Preheat the oven to 375°F, with a rack in the middle position.

**2.** Place the potatoes in a roasting pan and drizzle with the olive oil.

**3.** Bake until tender, 20 to 25 minutes.

**4.** Let the potatoes cool a little, 3 to 4 minutes, then smash them gently with the back of a wooden spoon.

**5.** Heat the vegetable oil in a large skillet over medium-high heat and fry the potatoes in batches until golden, turning once, 1 to 2 minutes per side.

**6.** Drain on paper towels. Sprinkle with salt and chives. Serve hot.

# Curried Potatoes

### Serves 4

3  pounds Yukon Gold potatoes
2  tablespoons butter
1  tablespoon extra-virgin olive oil
1  teaspoon curry powder
1  teaspoon sesame seeds
   Salt

**1.** Peel and dice the potatoes into ½-inch cubes.

**2.** Heat the butter and oil in a large skillet and add the potatoes, curry, and sesame seeds.

**3.** Cook the potatoes, stirring, over medium heat until lightly golden, about 15 minutes.

**4.** Season with salt and serve.

"EVERYTHING TURNS OUT WELL FOR GOOD BOYS." — PAUL LOWE

# Pavlova with Vanilla Cream & Blackberries

**Serves 4**

- 4 large egg whites
- 1 cup confectioners' sugar, plus more for sprinkling
- 2 tablespoons cornstarch
- 1 tablespoon white vinegar
- 1 teaspoon grated lemon zest
- 1 cup heavy cream
- ½ vanilla bean
- 2 cups fresh blackberries

When I was growing up, we had two desserts every Christmas Eve: cloudberries in whipped cream and Pavlova. I suspect the Pavlova came about because I don't like cloudberries, even though the sour little berries are an expensive delicacy in Norway.

A Pavlova is simple. It's a meringue baked in the oven and topped with cream and other goodies—a true treat that you can customize as you like. Try raspberries or strawberries, sliced peaches or nectarines, or roasted apricots or apples. Pavlova was named after a Russian ballet dancer. If I wore a tutu, would someone name a dessert after me?

**1.** Preheat the oven to 250°F, with a rack in the middle position. Line a baking sheet with parchment paper.

**2.** Beat the egg whites in a large bowl with an electric mixer until soft peaks form.

**3.** Beat in the confectioners' sugar, a little at a time, until you have firm peaks.

**4.** Add the cornstarch, vinegar, and lemon zest and stir well.

**5.** Pour the egg white mixture onto the baking sheet, using a spatula to even it out to form a circle.

**6.** Bake for 1 hour, rotating the pan from front to back after 30 minutes. Turn off the heat and let the meringue cool completely in the oven.

**7.** With a spatula, transfer the meringue to a serving dish.

**8.** Put the cream in a medium bowl and scrape the vanilla seeds into it. Dscard the vanilla pod. Beat to soft peaks with an electric mixer.

**9.** Spoon the whipped cream on top of the meringue.

**10.** Place the berries over the cream and serve right away.

# Lemon Tarts with Almond Crust

- 2 small lemons
- 2 cups plus 1 tablespoon granulated sugar
- 8 tablespoons (1 stick) cold butter, cut into pieces, plus more for the pan
- 1½ cups unbleached all-purpose flour
- ½ cup almond flour (available in health food stores)
- ½ teaspoon salt
- 1–2 tablespoons cold water
- 4 large eggs, plus 1 large egg yolk

Cover lemon slices with sugar, let sit overnight, and you'll wind up with lemon-scented syrup and softened slices that are as sweet as a lemon can be. The filling for these tarts, which are the perfect end to a meal, is nothing more than that syrup and eggs. The sophisticated taste is made even more special by the almond crust, and the color is divine.

You'll need to begin a day ahead of serving.

**1.** Slice the lemons into paper-thin slices, remove the seeds, and place in a medium bowl with 2 cups of the sugar.

**2.** Cover with plastic wrap and let sit at room temperature for at least 12 hours, preferably overnight.

**3.** Butter a 10-inch tart pan or four 3-inch tart pans.

**4.** Put the flour, almond flour, salt, the remaining 1 tablespoon sugar, and the butter in a large bowl.

**5.** Using your fingers, work the butter into the flour until the mixture is crumbly.

**6.** Mix 1 tablespoon water and the egg yolk in a small bowl, then mix it into the flour mixture. If the dough needs a little more water to come together (it should hold together when you pinch a bit), add the remaining 1 tablespoon water.

**7.** Press the dough into the tart pan(s) and refrigerate for 1 hour.

**8.** Preheat the oven to 375°F, with a rack in the middle position.

**9.** Prick the bottom of the dough with a fork. Place the tart pan on a baking sheet and bake for 15 minutes, or until the edges are light golden brown.

**10.** Remove the lemon slices from the sugar syrup and set aside. Add the eggs to the syrup, whisk well, and strain into a medium bowl.

**11.** Pour the egg mixture into the crust(s) and bake for 15 minutes, or until set.

**12.** Place 3 or 4 lemon slices on top of each small tart or 6 to 8 on the large tart.

**13.** Bake for another 15 minutes, or until the filling is set and lightly browned in spots.

**14.** Cool completely on a wire rack before serving.

# Chocolate & Salted Cashew Brittle Tart

## Makes one 10-inch tart; serves 8

10  tablespoons (1¼ sticks) butter, softened, plus more for the pan
½  cup plus 2 tablespoons confectioners' sugar
2  large egg yolks
1½  cups unbleached all-purpose flour
¼  cup unsweetened cocoa powder
¾  cup heavy cream
7  ounces bittersweet chocolate, chopped
1  cup packed light brown sugar
¼  cup granulated sugar
1  teaspoon Maldon sea salt
4  ounces cashews (½ cup)

Talk about decadent! I also call this tart "Jenny Craig's Worst Nightmare." The chocolate is key. The better the chocolate, the better the tart. But it doesn't stop there. Topping the creamy chocolate filling are shards of cashew brittle studded with flakes of salt. Maldon sea salt, from a small town outside London, is the finest finishing salt in the world.

You can also make the brittle on its own and serve it with cheese or as an addition to a green salad.

**1.** Butter a 10-inch tart pan.

**2.** Beat the butter and confectioners' sugar in a large bowl with an electric mixer until creamy, about 2 minutes.

**3.** Add the egg yolks and beat well.

**4.** Add the flour and cocoa and work it together well with your fingers or with the mixer on low speed.

**5.** Press the dough into the tart pan. Prick the bottom with a fork. Refrigerate for 1 hour.

**6.** Preheat the oven to 350°F, with a rack in the middle position.

**7.** Place the pan on a baking sheet and bake until the crust is golden and crisp, 12 to 15 minutes.

**8.** Cool on a wire rack.

**9.** Place the cream, chocolate, and brown sugar in the top of a double boiler or in a metal bowl set over simmering water and melt together.

**10.** Once the mixture is smooth, remove it from the heat and pour it into the tart shell. Refrigerate until set, about 2 hours.

**11.** Place the granulated sugar in a saucepan over medium heat and cook, stirring, until it becomes a golden caramel, about 10 minutes. Stir in the salt.

**12.** Line a baking sheet with parchment paper. Spread the cashews on it, pour the caramel over them, and let cool.

**13.** Remove the tart from the refrigerator 10 minutes before serving.

**14.** Break the brittle into pieces, place on top of the tart, and serve.

# World's Best Cake

## Serves 8

10½ tablespoons (1 stick plus 2½ tablespoons) butter, softened

1⅔ cups granulated sugar

1⅓ cups unbleached all-purpose flour

1 teaspoon baking powder

5 large eggs, separated

⅓ cup whole milk

¼ cup sliced almonds

1 cup heavy cream

½ vanilla bean

This cake was awarded the title of Norway's National Cake a few years back. It's called *verdens beste* in Norwegian, and I agree that it just might be the world's best. You may be skeptical of its superiority, since it isn't iced as are many American cakes. When we photographed it, I left it at the studio apartment of Alexandra Grablewski, this book's photographer, and the next day she confessed to having eaten two huge servings. "I guess the Norwegians are right," she said.

**1.** Preheat the oven to 350°F, with a rack in the middle position. Line an 8-x-12-inch baking pan with parchment paper.

**2.** Beat the butter and ⅔ cup of the sugar in a large bowl with an electric mixer until light and creamy, about 3 minutes.

**3.** Add the flour and baking powder and mix well on low speed.

**4.** Mix in the egg yolks and milk.

**5.** Scrape the batter into the baking pan.

**6.** In a large clean bowl, beat the egg whites and the remaining 1 cup sugar to soft peaks. Spread on top of the cake layer. Sprinkle with the almond slices.

**7.** Bake for 30 minutes, or until the meringue is golden brown and puffed. Cool on a wire rack in the pan. Transfer to a cutting board.

**8.** When the cake is cool, put the cream in a medium bowl and scrape in the vanilla seeds. Discard the vanilla pod. Beat to soft peaks with an electric mixer, about 3 minutes.

**9.** Cut the cake in half crosswise with a serrated knife. Place one half of the cake on a serving tray and cover with the cream. Place the other half, meringue side up, on top.

**10.** Let the cake sit for 1 hour in the fridge before serving.

# Tiramisu

## Serves 6

5 large eggs, separated, plus
   1 large egg yolk
¾ cup granulated sugar
1 (17-ounce) container
   mascarpone
1 cup strong brewed coffee, cold
¼ cup amaretto, or more to taste
24 packaged savoiardi cookies or
   ladyfingers
   Unsweetened cocoa powder, for
   sprinkling

I will gladly duel anyone who says that they have a better tiramisu recipe than me. Not with guns, but maybe a duel with cream pies? Certainly not a duel with this tiramisu—it's too good to waste! It's rich and dark with coffee and amaretto. Don't even think of trying it without the amaretto. You'll find savoiardi cookies (ladyfingers) in most supermarkets. If you like, make individual servings in six 3-inch ramekins.

Make the tiramisu ahead so that it can rest for at least 8 hours before serving. You'll be happy you did.

**1.** Beat the egg yolks and sugar in a large bowl with an electric mixer until pale yellow, about 2 minutes.

**2.** Beat in the mascarpone.

**3.** Beat the egg whites to soft peaks in another large clean bowl and gently fold into the mascarpone mixture.

**4.** Combine the coffee and amaretto in a small bowl.

**5.** Put a layer of 12 ladyfingers in a 9-inch serving dish and drizzle with half the coffee-amaretto mixture. Top with a thin layer of the mascarpone mixture. Layer the rest of the ladyfingers on top.

**6.** Drizzle with the rest of the coffee-amaretto mixture. Finish with a layer of the remaining mascarpone mixture.

**7.** Refrigerate for at least 8 hours or overnight.

**8.** Dust with the cocoa before serving.

# Norwegian Wood Cocktail

Serves 2

½  cup granulated sugar
½  cup water
6  raspberries
10  blueberries
4  blackberries
2  sprigs fresh rosemary
   Ice
   Juice of ½ lime
½  cup vodka
   Ginger ale

This is my homage to Norwegian forests, where we pick berries. Rosemary adds a piney note. The drink is very easy: Just muddle the berries and rosemary together and pour the other ingredients on top. Sometimes I make it in a pitcher, and when just the berries remain on the bottom, I fill it up with a cheap bottle of red wine and put it in the fridge. The next day, I have fresh sangria.

**1.** Combine the sugar and water in a small saucepan and bring to a boil, stirring until the sugar has dissolved, about 2 minutes. Refrigerate until cold, about 30 minutes.

**2.** Divide the berries and rosemary between two old-fashioned glasses.

**3.** Muddle well with the handle of a wooden spoon. Fill the glasses with ice.

**4.** Divide the chilled sugar syrup, lime juice, and vodka between the glasses and stir well.

**5.** Top with the ginger ale and serve.

# Jam Jar Vases

Jam jars are one of the most versatile craft supplies. I especially like the ones with fancy detailing that come in gift baskets.

## YOU WILL NEED:

River pebbles
Clean jam jars
Small orchid plants
Moss

**1.** Put some river pebbles in the bottom of the jars.

**2.** Transplant the orchids, keeping the original potting medium.

**3.** Cover with moss, then water the orchid.

# Bottles with Printout Flowers

## You will need:

Flower print outs (I download free
        images online from The
        Graphics Fairy; see Sources)
Scissors
Bamboo skewers
Glue
Old bottles

These little bud vases look supercute. I use old soda and liquor bottles that you can find at just about every flea market for pennies.

**1.** Cut the flowers out from the printout sheet.

**2.** Glue bamboo skewers onto the backs of the paper flowers to make stems.

**3.** Arrange them in the old bottles.

# Lace Votives

**YOU WILL NEED:**

Old lace
Votive holders
Scissors
Hot glue gun
Hot glue sticks
Votive candles

Tiny bits of old lace make these votives magical.

**1.** Wrap the lace around a votive holder to measure the length.

**2.** Cut the lace to the required length and place it so that it is not too near the flame of the votive.

**3.** Glue the lace into place with a dab of hot glue.

**4.** Drop in a votive candle. That's all!

"LIGHTING CANDLES EVERY NIGHT MAKES ME FEEL HAPPY." — PAUL LOWE

# Rope Votives

## You will need:

Hot glue gun
Hot glue sticks
Rope or cord
Jam jars or votive holders
Scissors
Votive candles

You can use whatever type of rope you'd like. I'm into neon, but natural cotton rope gives a more refined look.

**1.** Hot-glue the rope in a spiral around the jar, starting at the bottom.

**2.** Continue up the jar, alternating colors as desired, to about three-quarters up the sides.

**3.** Drop in a votive candle and enjoy.

# Candlesticks

## YOU WILL NEED:

Candles (I prefer regular to dripless, but cleanup can be an issue, so buy accordingly)

Metal nuts (make sure they are large enough to accommodate the candles)

Candles can set the mood for anything from a quiet supper at home alone to a boisterous dinner party. I keep a box of tapers handy, and my go-to candleholder is a simple metal nut from the hardware store. If you want to get fancy, you can buy one with a brass finish.

1. Insert the candles into the nuts.

2. Light the candles and enjoy.

My Hot Glue Gun

Hands down, my all-time favorite tool is the hot glue gun. I love it so much that I have one tattooed on my left arm. Talk about a serious crafter, eh? It's the most versatile tool ever. You can use it for countless craft projects, fixing jewelry, or repairing shoes—even assembling furniture. I have had the same one for eight years and it's beaten up and ugly, but I can't bear the thought that one day it will stop working. My partner jokes that when it finally gives up the ghost, he's going to have it bronzed for me. I just might take him up on the offer.

# Masterpiece Coasters

## You will need:

An old painting on canvas
Drinking glass
Pencil
Scissors

I can't pass up amateur artwork at thrift stores and flea markets, no matter how hard I try. These coasters take less-than-stellar artistry and turn it into something fun and useful.

1. Remove the canvas from the frame.

2. Place the drinking glass upside down on an interesting portion of the canvas and trace around the rim with the pencil.

3. Repeat for as many coasters as you'd like to make.

4. Cut the circles out from the canvas.

# Painted Chargers

## You will need:

Paint (I use enamel model paint,
   but you can even use leftover
   nail polish)
Paintbrush
Large plates or chargers (I use
   cheap white plates from a
   thrift store)

Chargers give a splash of color to any table setting.
This craft yields beautiful results without emptying your wallet.
If you're not using food-safe paint, don't eat off these plates and
be sure to hand-wash them.

**1.** Paint in broad strokes down the center of each charger.

**2.** Let dry and they're ready.

# Painted Runner

### YOU WILL NEED:

Roll of fabric-feel paper towels
    (such as Viva)
Fabric dye (I use Rit liquid dye)
Small bowls
Paintbrush

I make my own runners to match the occasion or the flowers that I'm using for a dinner party, since store-bought ones can be expensive and get stained from food or wine. You can throw this runner away after a use or two and create a new one for your next party.

**1.** Unroll the paper towels to the appropriate length for your table.

**2.** Pour the dye into bowls.

**3.** Using long brushstrokes, start to paint the runner, alternating colors as you like.

**4.** Let dry and it's ready to use.

# Swizzle Sticks

## YOU WILL NEED:

Large wooden beads
Paint
Paint brush
Wooden skewers or dowels that fit
    the holes in the beads
Wood glue or hot glue

Adding a swizzle stick makes even a glass of fizzy water seem festive. These giant ball swizzles give a space-age feel to cocktails or other refreshments.

**1.** Paint the wooden beads and let dry.

**2.** Glue a bead onto each skewer.

**3.** Raise your glass and say cheers!

# Box Clock

## You will need:

Cardboard gift box
Scissors or a large nail
Hot glue gun
Hot glue sticks
Clock kit (available online or at craft stores)

I keep a couple of clock kits on hand for last-minute projects. This project works well with Hermès boxes—I am very good at shopping at Hermès in the name of crafting—but you can turn any decorative box into a clock. Use a tea box for the kitchen or a Tiffany box for a blue bedroom. Jewelry boxes and handkerchief boxes also work well.

**1.** Make a small hole large enough to accommodate the armature of the clock kit in the center of the lid of the box with the scissors or a nail.

**2.** Glue the clock kit into place on the underside of the box lid.

**3.** Assemble the hands of the clock according to the manufacturer's instructions.

**4.** Close the box and display.

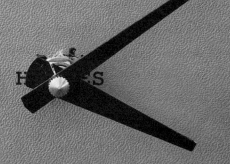

# Pie Tin Frame

## You will need:

Old pie tin
Photograph that will fit in the bottom
    of the tin
Pencil
Scissors
Hot glue gun
Hot glue sticks
Cotton rope

Old pie tins have a nice patina. I especially like the ones that are a little bit rusty. This project gives new life to tins too old for use in baking.

**1.** Place the pie tin over the section of the photo you want to frame.

**2.** Trace around the bottom of the tin with the pencil and cut out the photo.

**3.** Glue the photo to the inside bottom of the pie tin.

**4.** Glue a rope border around the photo for a beautiful vintage look.

# My Favorite Sources

These are some of my favorite stores and shops in New York City and beyond. Most of them will ship all over the United States and some even worldwide.

## Ribbons, Buttons & Embellishments
**M&J Trimming:** www.mjtrim.com
**Tinsel Trading:** www.tinseltrading.com
**Paper Mart:** www.papermart.com
**Hobby Lobby:** www.hobbylobby.com
**Pearl River Mart:** www.pearlriver.com
**Toho Shoji NY:** www.tohoshoji-ny.com
**Etsy:** www.etsy.com
**Mokuba:** www.mokubany.com

## Craft Supplies
**Michaels:** www.michaels.com
**Jo-Ann:** www.joann.com
**Lee's Art Shop:** www.leesartshop.com
**Amazon:** www.amazon.com
**Martha Stewart Crafts:** www.marthastewartcrafts.com
**Factory Direct Craft:** www.factorydirectcraft.com
**Tinsel Trading:** www.tinseltrading.com
**Oriental Trading:** www.orientaltrading.com
**A.C. Moore:** www.acmoore.com
**Etsy:** www.etsy.com
**Rit Dye:** www.ritdye.com

**Liquitex:** www.liquitex.com
**Dremel:** www.dremel.com
**Crayola:** www.crayola.com
**The Graphics Fairy:** www.thegraphicsfairy.com

## Paper & Packaging
**Annabel Gray:** www.annabelgray.etsy.com
**Garnish:** www.thinkgarnish.com
**Paper Presentation:** www.paperpresentation.com
**Paperchase:** www.paperchase.co.uk
**Lee's Art Shop:** www.leesartshop.com
**Paper Source:** www.paper-source.com
**The Container Store:** www.containerstore.com
**Kate's Paperie & Envelopes:** www.katespaperie.com
**Jam Paper:** www.jampaper.com

## Fabrics
**Skinny laMinx:** www.skinnylaminx.com
**Lotta Jansdotter:** www.jansdotter.com
**Jo-Ann Fabrics:** www.joann.com
**New York Elegant Fabrics:** www.nyelegantfabrics.com
**Mood Designer Fabrics:** www.moodfabrics.com
**Etsy:** www.etsy.com
**Gray Line Linen:** www.graylinelinen.com
**Marimekko:** www.marimekko.com
**Liberty:** www.liberty.co.uk

## Baking Supplies
**Bake It Pretty:** www.bakeitpretty.com
**New York Cake & Baking:** www.nycake.com
**Wilton:** www.wilton.com
**Williams-Sonoma:** www.williams-sonoma.com
**The Baker's Kitchen:** www.thebakerskitchen.net
**BakeryThings:** www.bakerythings.com
**Fancy Flours:** www.fancyflours.com
**Cookie Craft:** www.cookiecutters.com
**Amazon:** www.amazon.com
**Etsy:** www.etsy.com

## Yarn & Knitting
**Purl Soho:** www.purlsoho.com
**Yarn Market:** www.yarnmarket.com
**Habu Textiles:** www.habutextiles.com
**The Yarn Company:** www.theyarnco.com

## Inspiration & Props
**ABC Carpet & Home:** www.abchome.com
**Tinsel Trading:** www.tinseltrading.com
**Ochre:** www.ochre.net
**Jonathan Adler:** www.jonathanadler.com
**Steven Alan Home:** www.stevenalan.com/home
**Darr:** www.shopdarr.com
**Barneys:** www.barneys.com
**Anthropologie:** www.anthropologie.com
**Chelsea Market:** www.chelseamarket.com
**John Derian:** www.johnderian.com

**Red Chair Antiques:** www.redchair-antiques.com
**West Elm:** www.westelm.com
**West Elm Market:** www.westelmmarket.com
**Unionmade:** www.unionmadegoods.com
**The Mill:** www.themill.com
**Terrain:** www.shopterrain.com
**Designlump:** www.designlump.com
**Fishs Eddy:** www.fishseddy.com
**Brooklyn Flea:** www.brooklynflea.com
**West 25th Street Flea Market:** www.hells
kitchenfleamarket.com
**Greenhouse:** www.thegreenhouselifestyle.com
**Layla:** www.layla-bklyn.com
**eBay:** www.ebay.com
**Etsy:** www.etsy.com
**Brika:** www.brika.com

## Flowers
**Flower Muse:** www.flowermuse.com
**Terrain:** www.shopterrain.com

# Acknowledgments

It's easy to think that a book is made by the one person named on the cover, but the truth is far from it.

Ever since I moved to New York, I have worked with amazing talent and met some incredible people on the way.

The first is Alexandra Grablewski, who shot this book. You are a dream to work with, your use of light is stunning, and your way of working is easy.

I want to thank my team of assistants: Michaela Hayes, Meghan Farrell, and Courtney de Wet. I am grateful to Molly Rundberg, who tested my recipes.

Joline Rivera and Nellie Williams designed this beautiful book. I'm so happy with how it turned out.

There is another Paul behind Sweet Paul, Paul Vitale. I would not have been able to make this book without you and your support, your help on everything from the craft projects to the actual writing has been incredible.

A huge thanks to my agent, Judy Linden, and all the girls at Stonesong. You are my rock. I am so happy to have you in my life.

My editor, Rux Martin, at Houghton Mifflin Harcourt. You are amazing. It was love at first sight.

Also thanks to PropHAUS, Prop Workshop, Unionmade, Mill Mercantile, Designlump, Bubi Canal, and Todd Bonné.

And last but not least, my man, Anthony. Thanks for being understanding about my long hours in front of the computer.

I love you all.

Paul

# INDEX

Page numbers in *italics* indicate illustrations

NOTES

# NOTES